Spark & Hustle

SPARK & HUSTLE

Launch and Grow
Your Small Business Now

Tory Johnson

BERKLEY BOOKS, NEW YORK

BERKLEY BOOKS
Published by the Penguin Group
Penguin Group (USA) Inc.
375 Hudson Street, New York, New York 10014, USA
Penguin Group (Canada), 90 Eglinton Avenue East, Suite 700, Toronto, Ontario M4P 2Y3, Canada
(a division of Pearson Penguin Canada Inc.) • Penguin Books Ltd., 80 Strand, London WC2R 0RL,
England • Penguin Group Ireland, 25 St. Stephen's Green, Dublin 2, Ireland (a division of Penguin
Books Ltd.) • Penguin Group (Australia), 250 Camberwell Road, Camberwell, Victoria 3124, Australia
(a division of Pearson Australia Group Pty. Ltd.) • Penguin Books India Pvt. Ltd., 11 Community
Centre, Panchsheel Park, New Delhi—110 017, India • Penguin Group (NZ), 67 Apollo Drive,
Rosedale, Auckland 0632, New Zealand (a division of Pearson New Zealand Ltd.) • Penguin Books
(South Africa) (Pty.) Ltd., 24 Sturdee Avenue, Rosebank, Johannesburg 2196, South Africa

Penguin Books Ltd., Registered Offices: 80 Strand, London WC2R 0RL, England

This publication is designed to provide accurate and authoritative information in regard to the subject
matter covered. However, it is sold with the understanding that neither the author nor the publisher
is engaged in rendering legal, accounting, or other professional services. If you require legal advice
or other expert assistance, you should seek the services of a competent professional.

While the author has made every effort to provide accurate telephone numbers and Internet addresses at
the time of publication, neither the publisher nor the author is responsible for errors or for changes that
occur after publication. Further publisher does not have any control over and does not assume any
responsibility for author or third-party websites or their content.

PUBLISHING HISTORY
Berkley trade paperback edition: June 2012

Library of Congress Cataloging-in-Publication Data

Johnson, Tory.
Spark & hustle : launch and grow your small business now / Tory Johnson.—1st ed.
p.   cm.
ISBN 978-0-425-24746-4
1. New business enterprises.   2. Small business—Management.
I. Title.   II. Title: Spark and hustle.
HD62.5.J646 2012
658.1'1—dc23
2011050901

PRINTED IN THE UNITED STATES OF AMERICA

10 9 8 7 6 5 4 3 2 1

ALWAYS LEARNING   PEARSON

To every woman who dreams of creating a better life—
I'm rooting for you.

author's note

I'm a college dropout. I happily left school for a chance to begin my career at a young age. While I love books, I know you can't and shouldn't learn everything about life—especially the ins and outs of entrepreneurship—from them. That includes this one. On the following pages, I've given you my best advice, whether you're thinking about starting a business, have dipped your toes in the water, or are up and running. While I cover a lot, based on stuff I've learned along my own journey, it's up to you to pick and choose what you find useful. I don't pretend to be the definitive expert on how to start a business—just someone who loves this line of work. I've built two multimillion-dollar businesses, but nothing here is a substitute for legal or financial advice from professionals who can address your specific needs. If I could thrive as a small business owner—using the principles I've outlined here—you can, too.

contents

introduction

We both know why you're here.

You were downsized. Your hours were cut. Your employer went bust. You need to make more money to get by. You've graduated from college without a job and your career path isn't clear. You want to use your own smarts and creativity to take control of your working life.

You are like (and perhaps among) the thousands of people I meet at my Spark & Hustle conferences for current and aspiring entrepreneurs. While the ages span generations, and backgrounds are diverse at these events, one thing is clear: people are eager to make a change. Twentysomethings who abandoned job searches in favor of becoming their own boss. New moms who shudder at the thought of being beholden to a boss instead of their baby. Seasoned professionals who want to take the knowledge they gained on someone else's payroll to build their own venture. Employees who saw colleagues being fired and are determined to create a side business of their own. Retirees who dipped into savings to stay afloat and now must replace that income in their golden years.

We've all learned hard lessons in this new economy. The days of spending an entire career at one company, of a guaranteed paycheck with a pension to match are long gone. Job security, no matter how good you are at what you do, no longer exists. Many of us are still recovering from the downturn and anxious that storm clouds could gather again.

That's the end of the negativity you'll find in this book: being a naysayer won't get you far. Brighter days are most definitely ahead.

If the recession hit you hard or you were awakened by a reality check as peers were affected by a rough economy, it's time to strike back. That's the driving theme behind Diane Sawyer's ongoing "Made in America" series on ABC's *World News*, which has challenged ordinary people to renew their pride in all things American, to help keep jobs right here at home and revive our economy. I'm convinced that one of the best ways to do that is the old-fashioned American way: start your own business and produce goods and services right here in the USA.

We're entering a small business revival. The number of jobs may be stagnant, but the opportunities to launch a small business are not. In fact, small businesses drive most of the growth in our economy. By starting one, you can be part of the country's economic solution and, more importantly, your own.

Small business is booming because the barriers to starting one have never been lower. It's not a complicated or mysterious process to get going. Your computer can be your research and marketing department, even your storefront. Technology enables your corporate headquarters to be your kitchen table or corner coffee shop. A high-speed Web connection can be your road to success.

In July 2010, I held my first Spark & Hustle conference—spark for the ideas, passion and expertise that so many women have, hustle for what it takes to turn that into cash. For three scorching summer days in Atlanta, two hundred smart, savvy women shared their vision and dreams, while soaking up all kinds of tips and tactics from our roster of handpicked speakers—women who had started with nothing but guts and created successful businesses. They built their destinies brick by brick and shared their hard-won wisdom with others who wanted to do the same.

The feedback from the Atlanta event was so strong that I decided to take Spark & Hustle on the road. I wanted other women with established or fledgling businesses to learn from people who'd been there and done that—sometimes with the gray hairs to prove it.

I've spent the last year meeting thousands of talented current and would-be entrepreneurs at Spark & Hustle events in Atlanta, Boston, Chicago, Dallas, Houston, Los Angeles, New York, Orlando, Philadelphia and Tulsa.

What I learned from these women made writing this book possible and affirmed what I know to be true: desire and hustle trump education, experience and economics.

Forget the MBA. If you have one, great. But you don't need it; I'm a college dropout who launched a very successful business with very little money and no special connections. The women I work with are hungry to make things happen, but none of them have sugar daddies and I can't recall a single one saying she was born with a silver spoon in her mouth. They know it's all about the hustle: the decisions they make and the actions they take each and every day.

Now it's your turn to hustle.

I hope you're at least a tad crazy. It helps in this line of work.

At my Philadelphia Spark & Hustle event, maternity retail pioneer Liz Lange said, "Those of us who succeed do so because we're nuts." She's my kind of girl—making me feel normal (whatever that is) for being somewhat insane. This was a sentiment echoed on our stage by many of the most successful women today. Stella & Dot cofounder Jessica Herrin said it, too: "You have to be a little bit (or a lot) crazy to make it as a small business owner."

If you're OK with that—in fact, ready to embrace it—then let's make your business dream a reality. Only you can define what success looks like for you, but on these pages you'll learn what I did on my journey and what I've shared with others at my Spark & Hustle events: the nuts and bolts of starting and growing a profitable small business.

If there is a common trait among the women I meet who make it, it's this: they believe in themselves and what they are doing. That's the most potent fuel for an entrepreneur. Follow their lead and believe unflinchingly in yourself. And know that I'm rooting for your small business success.

CHAPTER ONE

||||||||||||||||||

spark & hustle

My "Why"

My entrepreneurial path began in 1990. An exciting summer internship, which ended with an entry-level job offer at ABC News, prompted me to quit college in favor of moving to New York City. From there I landed a position as a publicist at NBC News, promoting the network's superstars—Jane Pauley, Maria Shriver, the late Tim Russert, investigative ace Brian Ross, among others—and the programs they anchored. I loved the pace of breaking news, the thrill of working with the best in the business and the paycheck that afforded me, then a twenty-one-year-old kid, a decent lifestyle.

I was a solid performer—great at pitching and securing media coverage for NBC in the biggest newspapers, magazines and TV programs in the country. I loved what I did and where I did it—iconic 30 Rock—and I couldn't envision working anywhere else. NBC was home.

Then it all came apart. The newly appointed head of NBC News called me into his office. Sitting back in his big leather chair, hands clasped behind his balding head, he matter-of-factly explained that anytime someone takes over, change is inevitable. New protocols, new processes, new people . . .

It took me a few moments to catch on. I stammered, "Are you firing me?" His response was cold, bloodless: "You have thirty minutes to leave the building."

I wasn't ready to be fired without a fight. As a Florida state debate champ in high school, I had always been quick on my feet. I began rattling off my accomplishments, as well as a list of colleagues internally and externally who would vouch for me.

His response was a dull, blank stare.

I regrouped and suggested that he let me prove myself. "Give me three things to accomplish in three weeks, three months—whatever time frame you want."

He glanced at his watch.

It became clear there was no way I was going to change his mind. As I got up to walk out of his office, struggling not to lose it, he offered a parting thought.

"Tory, it's a big world out there, and I suggest you go explore it."

I didn't know it at the time, but that was some of the best advice I ever got professionally and personally. Yet in the moment, I was very tempted to tell him where he could take his exploration.

I spent months hiding in my apartment, shades closed. I hunkered down with Häagen-Dazs and daytime TV, filling my days and nights with self-doubt and panic. Venturing outside and meeting old friends or new people meant explaining my status. I knew how I had cringed when people said, "I'm in transition," or "I'm looking for my next opportunity." Losers. I didn't want anyone to think about *me* that way. My pity party turned into a misery marathon, financed by my severance pay, unemployment benefits and the 401(k) I stupidly cashed out because I figured it was easier than finding another job.

Between rent, ordering takeout and retail-clothing therapy, my cash vanished quickly—and I faced two choices: return home to Miami Beach, or snap out of it and find another job. Nothing wrong with Florida, but I wasn't going back. So I got out of my pajamas, picked up the phone, and eventually landed in corporate communications at Nickelodeon, the kids' cable network. I worked with fun people in a beautiful skyscraper overlooking Times Square. I had a nice office with a view, a six-figure salary, and I was all of twenty-three.

But that panicky feeling stuck with me—the one that comes from having been canned without warning.

I was *still* angry and hurt. I resented the notion that, despite my hard work, an arrogant man in a suit could take away my paycheck and, in the process, rob me of my dignity and self-worth. No matter how hard I tried, I couldn't shake it.

At the time, I thought my malaise stemmed from working for faceless corporations. So after three years at Nick, I decided to try something new: I accepted a marketing and public relations job for a start-up lifestyle magazine for twentysomethings.

We were a young, brash, enthusiastic staff on a mission: produce a glossy book that would change the world. This was a scrappy, entrepreneurial environment—no big expense accounts or fancy offices. None of that mattered because I was energized by the opportunity to be creative and resourceful in my new gig.

I did well there, but at some point my post-traumatic-pink-slip syndrome resurfaced. It wasn't something I thought about every day, yet the scary "what if?" always loomed. What if the magazine

folded? What if financing dried up? What if my position was eliminated? If you've ever had the rug pulled out from under you,
"what if?" takes on a whole new dimension. It can consume you.

I shared my "what if" worries with friends and family. The
advice was always the same: "Just keep doing a good job." "Make
sure the boss knows how hard you're working." "Keep your head
down and give it your best." I knew they meant well, and they
weren't wrong to say or think any of those things, but the conversation was very different in my head. Then another friend chimed
in with advice that hit a nerve. She said, "Stop worrying about
what you can't control."

That's the one that got me, which I'll never forget. I didn't *want*
to have to wonder if someone else would continue to find me a
valuable asset to the company. I didn't *want* to worry about protecting the status quo and building something, only to be sud-
denly canned again. I didn't *want* to have the threat of another
pink slip hanging over me. It was bad enough when I was younger.
But now I was a wife and mom: the stakes were much higher. The
idea that I couldn't control whether or not my paycheck was
steady weighed heavily.

It became obvious that I was never going to shake this pink-
slip scar while I was on someone else's payroll. I wanted to build
something on my own, bet on myself and see what I could do
with that same hustle I used every day to make someone else's
company thrive.

If I made the leap from the employment track to an entrepreneurial path, maybe that lingering layoff worry would begin to
heal. If I went out on my own, the "what if?" would turn into
"what's next?" Everything would be up to me. That concept is ter-
rifying for many people, but it was exhilarating to me.

So I quit the magazine, which was the most freeing personal

move I could have made. Ask anyone who has quit corporate America to go out on her own, and many will say the same thing.

I didn't quit to make more money or pursue a specific passion. My rationale for what so many people called a risky and irresponsible move was much deeper. I never, ever wanted my family to suffer as I had because of the impulse of a corporate exec. I wanted to provide my family with security that no one could take away. By founding and creating Women For Hire, a company that would produce career expos—pairing leading employers with professional women—we'd bank on *me*.

I told myself I couldn't go for it until I knew exactly what kind of business I'd create. For six months before going on my own, I thought day and night about how to start something based on my interest in promoting women, which stemmed from my admiration of the network news stars I had once worked with.

I found myself hanging out with my brother David's college friends, many of whom were women. This was just before their senior year at New York University. I expected tremendous excitement and enthusiasm about finishing up and getting out on their own. Instead, I learned they were anxious about landing jobs and launching careers. These were sophisticated girls: no lack of ego in this group. They were genuinely concerned about their ability to get in front of employers to beat the competition. If they felt this way, I could only imagine what was going on among students at less competitive schools.

So I began to envision creating a venue for bright women from all colleges and universities—not just the big ones—where they would feel comfortable and confident as they met face-to-face with top recruiters. In essence, I'd give them that foot in the door.

I made lists of the companies I wanted to attract to my events. I could see women walking through our doors in perfectly polished business attire, résumés in hand. I heard the buzz of the busy ballroom as hundreds of conversations took place amid the smiling faces and the exchange of business cards. I even scouted locations and got cost estimates from my top choices.

It was then that I had a very strong sense of what the business would be. With my focus sharpened, I put together my first career expo just three months after leaving that magazine job.

When I meet aspiring small business owners today, they're usually bursting with excitement over their big ideas. Their faces light up as they tell me about their incredible product or service. They envision customers lining up to buy. They can't wait to get going.

To these people I always ask one simple question: "Why? Why do you want to do this?"

Most times, the responses fall into the same categories: earning money, pursuing a passion, being their own boss and making the world a better place. All noble goals, of course, and I happen to share them. But I think to improve your odds for success, you need deeper and more personal motives. The further you dig, the closer you are to unlocking your true motivation.

Only when you own your "why" will you know you have that commitment to be ready, willing and able to tackle all the challenges that small business ownership will throw your way. That "why" is the fuel to keep you hustling.

What's *really* behind your desire to launch a business? Are you determined to insulate your family from the financial blow of a future pink slip? Do you want to control your time so you're more available for others? Have you sworn you'll never work for "the man" again? Do you believe that you could have greater influence and success by going out on your own?

Insulating my family from the repercussions of a corporate

decision was my initial impetus. So right before I started Women For Hire, I created a visual representation of my why. It was a heart-shaped poster with photos of my husband, Peter, and our kids. I laminated it at a copy shop. Looking at it every day was all I needed to stay on track, to focus on the big picture. Get out your photos and do the same thing when you discover your "why." Create a visual reminder and post it as your silent cheering squad to help you find focus and to fuel that fire in your belly.

I WANTED TO DO GOOD

For Christine Hutchison, who owns Chicago-based Five Accessories, five-accessories.com, which sells eco-friendly and fair-trade handbags, jewelry and home décor from Bali, Cambodia, India and Honduras, success means making a difference. "In Bali, on my honeymoon, a guide told me how much difference $5 a month can make there. Our first substantial donation was funding a school in Bali. I have a handwritten note from children trying to say 'thank you' in English."

From "Why" to "When"

Women ask me all the time, "When should I quit my day job and work on my business full-time?"

Some people just up and quit. Others start their businesses on the side and keep their day jobs. There are many options in between, of course, and no single path fits all. Emily Bennington spent two years working after hours on her business-consulting practice, Professional Studio 365, before making the full-time leap. She was a successful marketing leader at a Top 10 accounting firm, known for generating creative ideas to help new hires thrive at a competitive company. Higher-ups praised her work, but they rarely allowed Emily to actually put her ideas into action. Instead, they hired consultants to swoop in to execute them. Time and again, she watched from the sidelines as those ideas came to life. Finally, she'd had enough. Her passion for her work was too strong to allow others to do what she craved.

But Emily also had a family. She had bills to pay and didn't feel that she could leave her job without having steady income to replace her paycheck. So she chose to work at her business on the side. She used vacation days to give speeches and attend conferences, spent evenings writing a book and, yes, stole spare moments at her day job to post blog entries and correspond with key contacts using her personal email.

It was after Emily attended a 2011 Spark & Hustle conference in New York that she says she was inspired to make the leap and leave her full-time job earlier than she had originally planned. She learned from the other women there that it's much harder to grow a business on the side than when you throw yourself into it 24/7.

Her original goal was to replace her salary, but when she hit half that per month by doing side projects, she knew it was time to leave. After months of cutting her expenses and squirreling away money in savings, a nervous but determined Emily went for it. Her must-haves included health insurance, a few regular clients, a great website and affordable day care.

Today, employers call on Emily to teach them how to recruit and retain the best entry-level talent. At human resource conferences, she shows companies how to develop programs to help new hires succeed. She gives speeches on college campuses and at women's events about how to be a rock star on the job. Emily also writes extensively and pitches herself to the media as a college-to-career expert, which has generated national attention for her work, along with clients and referrals. Emily's doing what she does best: getting paid to generate ideas and programs that inspire others.

Be an Emily. Don't wait for someone else to tell you what to do. You have to make the decision based on your financial situation, personal circumstances and ability to handle uncertainty. Financial guru Suze Orman has said you should have twelve months of operating expenses in the bank before launching a business. I love Suze, but that's not very realistic for most aspiring entrepreneurs. If I had waited until I could bank even half of that before starting Women For Hire, I would never have gotten it off the ground. I barely had a couple of months of cash when I took the plunge. My guess is that most entrepreneurs are in the same boat—I know the ones I work closely with sure are.

SUCCESS TAKES TIME

Instant is the exception, not the rule, says Deborah Shane (deborahshane .com), a Fort Lauderdale, Florida, consultant who advises small business owners. "Most successful entrepreneurs I know are ten-year overnight successes. Pace yourself and be patient with growth and progress."

healthy coverage

If you don't have access to health insurance, check first with your most recent carrier to determine if you're eligible for an individual policy. Quick policy and price comparisons can be found at ehealthinsurance.com, but your options don't stop there. Explore plans through your state's Department of Labor. Ask other small business owners for introductions to health insurance brokers who can source policies for you.

Figure out what you need—what's "good enough"—to take the next step. Maybe it's a certain amount of cash you want in savings. Maybe it's a minimum number of clients ready to go. Maybe it's receipt of a year-end bonus. Maybe it's just a matter of setting the date and pulling the trigger. Once you identify what it is, work toward making that happen.

BEATING BAG LADY SYNDROME

Women on Fire founder Debbie Phillips (debbiephillips.com) says "bag lady syndrome," the common fear of losing everything and literally being out on the street, is the first emotional and mental stage of entrepreneurship, often felt by women stepping off the corporate ladder and carving out work of their own. At Spark & Hustle Orlando, Debbie said her antidote to this is patience. "Dive into the daily work of building your life and business. Wrap yourself with inspiration, expert strategies and lots of support. Keep moving forward. If you will do that, you will discover you'd rather be a bag lady than to give up what you've built."

Here's a quick checklist to get started:

_____ Savings to satisfy your sanity

_____ Child care or elder care arrangements

_____ Affordable health insurance

_____ Personal support network

_____ Other based on your personal preferences

DO IT DIFFERENTLY

Don't be afraid to run your business differently, says Sandy Stein, a former flight attendant who founded Alexx Inc., which manufactures and markets patented Finders Key Purse (finderskeypurse.com), a small gadget that prevents keys from being lost at the bottom of your bag. When she couldn't convince traditional product reps to shop her line to retailers, she enlisted other flight attendants to introduce it to boutique owners in their hometowns on their off days. That's how Sandy secured distribution in thousands of stores nationwide. "If I had waited for 'normal' distribution as others had done, I would not be in business today."

Reality Check

There is value in dreaming big, imagining what you want your life and business to be, turning that vision into a plan and then going for it. That's exactly what I want this book to help you do. But first, a few ground rules.

THINK LIKE AN IMMIGRANT

I live in New York, a city of immigrants. New York has always welcomed people from other countries and it's hard to imagine it any other way. Another thing I can't imagine is anything more frightening than landing alone in a foreign country, not speaking the language, having no money and not knowing anyone. Yet that's exactly what the first two babysitters we hired for Jake and Emma did when they emigrated from Russia to New York. Veronika and then Cici, who cared for my kids from two months to age twelve, arrived at different times from the Ukraine and Georgia, each with a suitcase, a few hundred dollars, no plan for where they might live and not speaking more than a few words of English.

Today, Veronika has a solid job bidding on contracts for a large construction company in Massachusetts, tapping into the engineering degree she earned back home. Cici just got her master's degree in speech therapy and has a private practice. They both speak fluent English. They're both among the hardest working women I know.

Why? Because they have a "whatever it takes" work ethic. No task was ever beneath them, no hours too long, nothing taken for granted.

Here in Manhattan, I witness that immigrant mentality routinely because I'm surrounded by newcomers. Chinese grocers whose shops never close. The same delivery guy from Ecuador who shows up at my door in the morning when the kids want bagels for breakfast and at night when they order a snack. Ditto for the newsstand guy from Bangladesh and Amanda, the Korean woman at my dry cleaners who works 6 A.M. to 8 P.M. Monday to Saturday, fifty-two weeks a year.

EMBRACE RISKY THINKING

Ross Kimbarovsky, cofounder of crowdSPRING (crowdspring.com), a crowd-sourcing logo and graphic design community, says that when you face risk, "you start thinking differently." A small business owner thinks differently from someone whose livelihood isn't on the line every day. Every dollar of that business owner's profit feeds his or her family and helps put a roof over the family's head. Such a business owner is constantly at risk. Ross told Spark & Hustle in Boston that to be in small business you have to be OK with that and comfortable with the fact that you'll think differently from people in the nine-to-five world.

You could say they work such long hours because they have to—to make ends meet—and that's probably true. But I also think many of them are driven to succeed, to triumph over whatever adversity has been thrown their way, because the alternative is too dark to imagine.

For me, returning to the corporate world represents that darkness—it's what fuels me every day to push to succeed, along with knowing that other people in my life depend on me. Perhaps my mentality is a bit stark, but most successful entrepreneurs I know have some variation of it. They work as if their lives depend on it. They genuinely do whatever it takes.

Yet I've spoken with scores of business-owners-to-be who say they want to set up shop to have more leisure time. They describe making their own schedule, having plenty of free time, and a life with money, freedom and no boss. All of this is possible, of course, but don't underestimate the initial and ongoing commitment of your time and the sheer number of hours you will work to turn a profit.

Being a business owner can make you more money, give you more freedom than you've ever had before, and allow you to design your life according to your preferences. Travel or no travel; set up at home or in an office; work alone or as part of a team. If being an entrepreneur didn't afford my family and me the life it does, I wouldn't do it.

But I have never worked more hours than I do now. It took years of struggle and sacrifice—long hours, typically seven days a week—to make my business a big moneymaker. And it's an ongoing devil. I still work harder than I ever did at one of my "real" jobs. Once again, talk to most entrepreneurs and they'll echo this.

Call me crazy, but I wake up each morning ready to tackle a

new day and a new set of challenges. I'm even more thrilled that I chose this path than as I was on Day One.

JOY BEHIND THE LONG HOURS

Karen Young, owner of Hammocks & High Tea (hammocksandhightea .com), a Brooklyn, New York, textile and product-design studio, says she can't recall a single job "where I felt more like myself than I do every day now. The hours are long, but the joy at what I do far outweighs it."

Pluck vs. Luck

I learned the word *pluck* from my father-in-law, Jim Johnson. He used to call me "plucky," and I had to look it up because it sounded like a name for a chicken. It means "determined, daring, fearless, spirited, resolute, audacious, spunky, unflinching, gutsy." I love it. Pluck is the very definition of what it takes to be a profitable small business owner.

Women often tell me how *lucky* I am to own a successful small business. It's true: I have had good fortune, but it has come from hard work and determination. *Luck* is rare and unreliable. *Pluck* is the very opposite. It's about taking control and making your goal a reality. I'll take pluck over luck every time.

No one would say that Tierra Destiny Reid was lucky when Macy's eliminated her department while she was on maternity leave in 2009. Instead of looking for another job, she decided to start a business. A stylish woman on a military wife's budget, Tierra knew from experience how to stay fashionable at a discount.

It took pluck to take what she knew about budget fashion and turn it into a profitable retail operation. She scoped out the right location, negotiated a favorable lease, furnished the space with used fixtures and opened a clothing store that is now Stylish Consignments, a go-to resale resource in Atlanta.

Tierra invested every penny of her $6,000 in severance and ended the year grossing $80,000 in retail sales—without incurring a dime of debt. (I'll talk more about avoiding debt in the coming chapters.)

Some people are born with pluck, but others have to learn how to take risks and see them through. You'll need pluck to deal with the adversity and opportunity that you'll encounter along the way. You may dream of catching lightning in a bottle, but never count on it. Don't expect to get lucky, either.

Mistakes Happen

I've made more mistakes than I care to count, but I rarely make the same one twice. My career expos originally ran from 10 A.M. to 6 P.M. I figured that by spending more than $2,000 a pop for a recruiting booth, HR reps would expect an eight-hour expo to get their money's worth. What I found, however, was that by about 3 P.M., the pace of arrivals among job-seekers had come to a complete stop, and the ballroom was dead for the remainder of the afternoon, which meant events ended on a downer. Not a good thing. But I worried about reducing the hours without having to reduce the cost to employers. Ultimately, I realized that cutting back hours delivered the same number of candidates, but more efficiently. The events now wrap at 2 P.M. and my booth rates are the same.

I also wasted time and money on event booklets for attendees.

My mom and I worked hours and hours at Kinko's, formatting ads from each participating employer, trying to get them all just right. Since neither of us is a graphic designer, or familiar with how to do this on a computer, it was difficult and stressful. Worse, nobody seemed to read our fancy handouts. Today, we print a short paragraph on each employer in a Word document. It works just fine.

The majority of my early mistakes are more universal to most small business owners: inefficient bookkeeping and poor hiring decisions, probably because I wasn't good at or interested in those things. My passion was (and still is) focused on women's career issues, not the nitty-gritty of running a business. I learned to get help in those areas where I knew I lacked the necessary knowledge, and I forced myself to get skilled in finances since it became essential to growing the business.

I first met Michael Alter, president of SurePayroll, as a client. His company is the leading online payroll services company and serves Women For Hire and more than thirty-five thousand other small businesses. I got to know Michael better because his company sponsors Spark & Hustle conferences, where he has shared with my attendees lessons on business success and failure.

"Mistakes are the tuition you pay for success," he says. In fact, SurePayroll gives out a "Best New Mistake Award" to an em-

NO EASY ROUTE

Adversity is part of the deal in small business, says Maria Peagler, operator of SocialMediaOnlineClasses.com, which offers social media training. "There is no such thing as a perfect or easy route to success," she says. "You have to fail first and often before you can succeed. Beethoven changed his symphonies sixty or seventy times before they were complete."

ployee annually because Michael believes that fear of making a mistake is the same as fear of success. No risk, no reward. (There's no award at SurePayroll for making the same mistake twice.)

Michael says fear of making a mistake will halt your vision and your company's progress. "The longer you wait to try something new, the longer you'll wait to learn something your competitors might already know." Learn from it, correct it quickly and move on.

To illustrate his point, Michael talks about teaching his kids to walk. All of them fell, bumped their head and got bruised. One even made a trip to the emergency room. But they survived and today Michael is proud to say all three of his kids walk perfectly.

Getting a handle on what it takes to run your business will mean you stumble from time to time. Get up, dust yourself off and find your way.

"Fear Sucks!"

As the workplace contributor on ABC's *Good Morning America*, I once did a story on a woman whose fear paralyzed her job search. She met with a coach who showed her a Harley-Davidson motorcycle ad that read:

> Over the last 105 years in the saddle, we've seen wars, conflicts, depression, recession, resistance and revolution. We've watched a thousand hand-wringing pundits disappear in our rear-view mirror. But every time this country has come out stronger than before. Because chrome and asphalt put distance between you and whatever the world can throw at you. Freedom and wind

outlast hard times. And the rumble of an engine drowns out all the spin on the evening news. If 105 years have proved one thing, it's that fear sucks and it doesn't last long. So screw it, let's ride.

The same is true for your business. The "chrome and asphalt [that] put distance between you and whatever the world can throw at you" are your pluck and planning. Face fear with determination and action, knowing your passion and hard work will outlast hard times. The rumble of your need to succeed will drown out naysayers and negativity.

Since that segment on *GMA*, I've worked with thousands of business owners who regularly bring up fear as an obstacle to business growth. They're afraid that they're investing too much in a pipe dream. They're afraid that the bills will come due before the money comes in, that they've missed their chance or will hit the market before they are ready. They're afraid of large competitors outmarketing them and smaller competitors underpricing them, that they're not good enough to make great things happen. The list is endless.

Fear comes with the territory. For most of us—and I'm no exception—all safety nets are gone. I get it. But I refuse to let fear

HOW WILL YOU KNOW?

Ara Farnam, owner of Rock Paper Scissors (rpscissors.com), an events company in New York, says there have been times when she wasn't confident her business was going to work. "I applied for a job once in a moment of weakness. I knew I really wanted to make my business work because my reaction to [getting] the job was disappointment and anxiety—and it was a great job."

stop me from aggressively pursuing business opportunities. I've accepted fear as part of the deal. It does not go away, but it does not have to own you.

Listen to your fear, challenge it, use it to get started and move forward. When you fear running out of money, analyze your spending and justify all expenses. When you fear giving a pitch to prospective clients, practice it so extensively that you can look at yourself in the mirror and say: *Nobody knows this better than I do.* When you fear hearing no, rehearse your responses and remember: you can't win every time. Don't allow fear to paralyze you. Pay attention to the root of it and then act. Action is the enemy of fear.

Keep fear in perspective, too, says another Spark & Hustle speaker, Jess Weiner, Dove's global self-esteem ambassador, who teaches women how to harness their confidence. "Fear," she says, "is often a down payment on a debt you may not owe."

So in the words of Harley-Davidson: Screw it, let's ride.

ⅢⅢ act now ⅢⅢⅢⅢⅢⅢⅢⅢⅢⅢⅢⅢⅢⅢⅢⅢⅢⅢⅢⅢⅢⅢⅢⅢⅢⅢⅢⅢⅢⅢⅢⅢⅢⅢⅢⅢⅢⅢ

- Small business is booming because the barriers to starting one have never been lower. Everyone has easy access to technology. Your computer can be your research and marketing department, even your storefront. There are countless resources to support your efforts. And, let's face it, it's cool to start and own a thriving small business right now.

- Determine what's behind your desire to launch a business. Only when you own your "why" will you know that you're ready, willing and able to tackle all the challenges that small business ownership will throw your way.

- Know your must-haves for getting started and for making your business a full-time endeavor.

- Don't underestimate the initial and ongoing commitment of your time to turn a profit.

- Anticipate how you will manage the uncertainties. List three to five of your biggest fears and how you'll take action to prevent them from paralyzing you.

CHAPTER TWO

||||||||||||||||||

discovering your spark

While your "why" is your motivator, your spark is the heart of your business. Your spark fills your thoughts during the day and keeps you awake at night. If you're lucky, it's the thing you're most qualified to do based on your skills, knowledge and expertise. It's what you're crazy about. Combine your spark with some hustle and you have a winning formula.

But some would-be entrepreneurs only have one, not the other. Take the accountant who is brilliant with numbers, but if she has to audit another balance sheet or prepare another tax return, she'll lose her mind. The skill is there, but the passion is not. She dreams instead of opening a garden shop that stocks a beautiful assortment of flowering plants, though she lacks a garden of her own. As long as she's committed to learning this new trade, there's no reason why this business can't be successful. It may just take a bit longer—and present more growing pains—than a business built on existing skill and passion.

When I launched Women For Hire, I knew nothing about selling to human resource professionals or planning and executing large recruiting events. But I knew my marketing and PR skills—combined with enough determination to make pigs fly—would allow me to overcome my lack of experience in sales. I also knew my interest in promoting women, which originated during my competitive years in high school debate when all of my opponents were guys, and grew stronger while I worked for some of the most powerful women in America, including Barbara Walters, Maria Shriver and Jane Pauley, would lead me to figure out how to learn whatever I needed to know along the way.

LACK OF EXPERIENCE CAN BE A PLUS

Not knowing much about the food business actually worked in her favor, says Colette Cyrus-Burnett, who owns Super Wings (mysuperwings.com) in Brooklyn, New York, specializing in Caribbean-flavored chicken wings. "I went forward sure that I could accomplish anything," Colette says. "I was convinced that if I worked hard, made a consistently excellent product and treated people like I wished to be treated, I could win. Acknowledging my lack of experience gave me empathy for my team, which helped build a culture of compassion. We are good at helping each other grow." Plus, she says, had she known how challenging it would be to get the business going, Colette might have been too scared to start.

Your spark probably exists inside you already. But the daily grind, fear and uncertainty can make it hard to recall or find. Most people talk about career reinvention. I like to think of professional evolution, which builds on bits and pieces of all of your endeavors and leads you in new directions. You may very well know you're ready for something new, but not yet know what your next progression is going to be. Don't fret, though, as your ideas and experiences will no doubt lead to that discovery. If you aren't sure what your spark might be, read on. But if you've determined your spark, then jump ahead to "Fanning the Flames" on page 39.

Ultimately, if you dream of being on your own but haven't found your spark, you have to trust your head and heart to guide you to the right place. A healthy dose of your own instinct helps, too. So take some time—perhaps a few hours, maybe even a few weeks, months, or even longer—to consider some key questions, which will help to reveal *your* spark.

Retrain Your Brain and Capture Your Calling

For many would-be small business owners, the dream dies because of seemingly insurmountable real or imagined obstacles. Maybe you've even done this at one time or another—pushed your hopes to the back burner because you thought you lacked the means—time, money, education, connections or *whatever*—to make your vision come alive. And that puts you back to square one again and again.

The truth is you can always find obstacles no matter what you're doing, unless you simply refuse to allow them to obstruct you. Allow yourself to think as big as you can. Don't eliminate anything simply because you see roadblocks. Making this cognitive shift may take time and retraining on your part because you might have spent so many years beating down ideas when you doubted your ability to overcome inevitable challenges. As such, clearing your head of all that negativity may be easier said than done. Keep at it. Focus on what's possible. Norman Vincent Peale's iconic *The Power of Positive Thinking* isn't an international best seller for nothing.

Is there risk in taking on something new, the unknown? In not knowing exactly what lies ahead? Of course. But risk is something we all face every day when we decide to get out of bed, leave home and do *anything* in life—whether it's going to work, the mall or out to dinner. Do you typically think of all the *bad* things that might happen to you when you head out each morning? Of course not. Adopt that same spirit when you're thinking about *what could be*.

Once you've opened your mind to possibility, begin the big brainstorm to capture your calling. Make time to get comfortable. Put on your favorite outfit, make your most enjoyable snack, play inspiring music and settle in as you answer some questions. Don't overthink it and don't allow perceived obstacles to prevent you from giving honest answers. There's no right or wrong here.

1. a. What do most people who know you really well say you're good at?
   b. What hobby or activity do you most enjoy?

2. a. What would you say you're good at?
   b. If you could do anything for a week, what would you do?

3. a. What skill or expertise do friends and family always turn to you for?
   b. In what category would you earn a blue ribbon, gold medal and every other top prize?

4. a. As a child, what did you want to be when you grew up?
   b. In the last five years, what do you remember dreaming about doing professionally?

5. a. If you could create your own how-to website or write your own how-to book, what topic would you tackle?

b. If you did not need to make money, what would you do
professionally?

Compare and Eliminate

Hopefully, your answers have revealed interesting ideas and possibilities. Now narrow down your responses. Look back at your
answers to questions A and B in number one. Which would you
rather pursue right now if you had to pick one? Circle it.

Now do the same for your A and B responses to questions two
through five. Which of the two is more desirable at this moment?

You should have five circled answers. Eliminate two of the options, leaving just three of the original ten. Those final responses
may be very similar—or you can probably identify common
themes among them.

Congratulations: you've begun the initial steps to pinpointing
your calling. This is likely among the things that makes your
heart soar, even if you're not yet sure how it may line your bank
account. We'll get to the money part eventually, but this stage is
about identifying what excites you enough to do it day and night,
no matter what obstacles show up.

You're on your way. The rest of these exercises should focus on
your top choice among the responses you just revealed.

Pursuit of Preferences

Answer the following questions, then use the key to encourage
a greater understanding of your likes and dislikes. There are no
right or wrong answers here, either, so respond truthfully. If you
answer against your genuine feelings, you'll cheat yourself out of
potentially discovering the path that's a fit for you.

1. Do you like trailblazing new ideas or would you rather put your own spin on something that's been proven to work before?

    If you answered yes to trailblazing new ideas, bravo. Since an exact roadmap won't exist, study the stories of other small business owners who have pioneered something in their respective fields, to gain insight on some of the challenging aspects of creating an entirely new offering.

    If you indicated that you'd prefer to put your own spin on something that's been proven to work before, don't feel discouraged when you see similar offerings out there. Instead, celebrate—it means there's a market already in place. We know that an endless number of coffee shops and coaching practices can happily coexist quite successfully without reinventing the wheel. Similarly, thousands of direct sellers successfully coexist within the same companies. Focus on what makes you different—what your unique twist will be—and go from there.

2. Do you like working one-on-one with customers for long periods of time, seeing gradual results, or do you prefer short, quick transactions with instant results?

    This answer is especially relevant when considering your product or service offering, target customer and sales process. If you prefer short, quick transactions, you may sell a ready-made product online that requires little if any customer interaction. If you're a fashion designer, you'd stick to off-the-rack, not customized, clothing or accessories. A fitness trainer who wants quick transactions might provide her services through a hotel gym where she'll see transient guests, but a trainer who values long-term relationships is better suited to helping clients get in shape over an extended period of time.

3. Do you like working solo—making all business decisions and completing every task on your own? Or do you envision employing other people, letting them into your business, delegating tasks and responsibilities?

   If you want to work alone, choose something that does not require more work than you're willing and able to accomplish. Of course, you'll put in a lot of hours anyway as a small business owner, but stretching yourself too thin is a killer. There is nothing wrong with aiming small. Not every small business owner's goal is to be big. True success is maintaining a size that's manageable for you and generates enough income to support your desired lifestyle.

   While I never set out to have a staff, the financial goals I set for my business as it evolved required me to shift from solo operator to hiring several employees. The workload demanded as much.

4. Do you want to leave your mark on the world or are you mainly focused on making a living doing something you like to do?

   Creating a legacy from your life's work is a noble goal, but your business doesn't need to save humanity if that's not what matters most to you. Some of us are keen on making a difference, while most people are perfectly content to do an honest day's work, fulfill a service or a need and pay the bills. Nothing wrong with either choice; it's yours to make, but it should figure into your business planning equation. Neither choice is mutually exclusive. You can do well (in business) by doing good (for society) if that's what excites you.

Perceived Obstacles

It's OK to see obstacles in the way of a new pursuit as long as you don't allow them to derail your efforts. Instead of focusing on what you can't do, think about how to overcome whatever stands in your way.

But for now, let's assume that you've fallen into the trap of seeing all kinds of challenges. What to do?

First, think about the calling you identified in the first series of questions. Say, for example, you're a fashionista who dreams of launching a luxury line of leather handbags. Use the space below to list ten perceived obstacles. If you end up with fewer, beautiful. If you end up with more, that's OK, too.

Maybe the roadblocks in your mind include any of the following: You lack formal design training. You've never sewn. You have no clue where or how you'd source leather. You lack the funds to buy the supplies. You're worried that it's a very crowded field with absolutely no shortage of handbag options for women.

1. _____

_____

_____

2. _____

_____

_____

3. _____

_____

_____

4. _____

_____

_____

5. _____

_____

_____

6. _____

_____

_____

7. _____

_____

_____

8. _____

_____

_____

9. _____

_____

_____

10. _____

_____

_____

Now get ready to wash away the excuses.

Step Outside the Box

Look back at these answers and prepare to argue against each of them. This will take effort, especially since you've just convinced yourself of the validity of what stands in your way. Push yourself—and your thinking. Pretend you're helping your best friend get over a fear. Tap your inner Superwoman—that voice that says, "I can do anything I set my mind to."

To get started, look at my example:

The fashion lover who wants to launch a handbag line believes these things stand in her way:

OBSTACLE #1: Lack of formal design training

SOLUTION #1:
Take a course at a community college. Watch YouTube videos on how to design handbags. Find a mentor, including a current design student, who has done this before and can show you the ropes. Break down the necessary steps and use your transferable skills to figure it out as you go.

OBSTACLE #2: No sewing skills

SOLUTION #2:
Learn how to sew, which you could probably figure out within a few days. Hire someone on a per-piece basis to sew your bags.

**OBSTACLE #3: Lack of knowledge on
how to source for leather**

SOLUTION #3:

Google "leather suppliers" and cold-call a dozen companies to ask for sample swatches and pricing. Ask another business owner who uses leather for a noncompetitive product such as shoes, clothing or even dog carriers to provide you with leads. Contact your chamber of commerce for help identifying manufacturers in your area. Read articles online on how to select an ideal supplier for your materials or a manufacturer for your product.

OBSTACLE #4: Lack of funds for supplies

SOLUTION #4:

Determine the minimum amount of cash or credit you need to produce your first set of samples. Use those samples to score an order, for which you can require a deposit to be used toward the purchase of the necessary supplies. Create samples and host a trunk show where you take orders and deposits before producing the goods. Barter or borrow the minimum amount of money to get started from someone who would likely be a buyer of your line. You get her cash and she gets first dibs on your new pieces.

OBSTACLE #5: Crowded marketplace

SOLUTION #5:

Great! Women love handbags, so we're in heaven with an endless array of options. Many women love discovering new designers, so those people will become part of your target market. Large retailers are always on the hunt for the next big thing, while small boutiques look for lesser-known lines to differentiate their merchandise from the retail giants.

Get the idea? Forcing yourself to look beyond the obvious problems will help you discover workable solutions. Once you complete all of these exercises, you should feel more clear and confident about your potential business idea.

THE PERFECT FIT

While pregnant with her first child, Vanessa Wilson began making patterns and sewing pieces for her baby. Friends asked her to teach them how to make the same items, so she created video tutorials and posted them on YouTube. What started as a hobby took off as others found her work. She formed the Crafty Gemini (craftygemini.com), discovered that she could make money creating and selling sewing patterns online, and in the process became a celebrated YouTube star. Vanessa has built an impressive following and sizable income doing what she loves even though she never set out to pursue this as a career.

Consider the Big Picture

While growing up in Miami Beach, I was a high school debater who dreamed of being on TV. I had no clue what I'd say or do on TV, but it was on my mind. My inspirations were Oprah and Barbara Walters.

My first step toward fulfilling that vision was successfully pursuing an internship at ABC News' *20/20* after my freshman year at Emerson College. I moved to New York for the summer and lived above a smelly restaurant on the Upper West Side. I was blown away when I got to meet Barbara and help promote her newsmaker interviews. So much so that I jumped at the chance to intern there again the next summer. When a vacancy opened, I dropped out of school for a full-time job in public relations at the show. That led to a communications role at NBC News.

Years later, when I started my own business, I used all of that PR savvy to promote Women For Hire and attract attendees to my career expos. I booked myself on radio and TV and began drawing on my ideas and public speaking skills to offer other women career advice. This wasn't about my ego; it was a necessity to promote my events when I had zero dollars for advertising. But the TV bug bit hard about five years into it when I landed my first *Good Morning America* segment. Piece by piece over time, I merged that early dream of being on TV with the business I'd built serving women in their careers, even though I could never have predicted this particular path from Day One. In retrospect the signs

PR BY BARBARA

I learned public relations from the very best in the business: Barbara Walters and her handpicked publicist Maurie Perl, my then-boss at ABC News, who now heads communications for publishing powerhouse Condé Nast, publishers of iconic magazines including *Vogue*, *Glamour*, *GQ* and more. In a nutshell, the rule of thumb when seeking media coverage is to have something newsworthy that people will care about and to learn who covers your beat. Get to know those reporters by name and make contact even when you don't need anything. This is what I did with the workplace beat when I launched Women For Hire. I made it my business to become friendly with reporters who covered women's careers. I became a trusted source with a fresh perspective, and I suggested story ideas that often didn't include me. This led to exceptional, sustained coverage, which ultimately helped build my profile and my business.

were there, which is what I hope you see in your answers on the previous pages.

Cindy W. Morrison didn't wake up one morning with an epiphany about the business she would build. Quite the contrary. She says she planned to retire as an award-winning TV news anchor in Tulsa, Oklahoma, after her third face-lift (her words, not mine). But on the cusp of turning forty and in her career prime, Cindy's boss gave her the bad news: he wasn't renewing her contract. She was out.

After her pink slip, Cindy poured her soul into writing *Girlfriends 2.0*, a book honoring the women who supported and encouraged her during this transition. She self-published and sold more copies in a month than many authors sell in a lifetime. Her not-so-secret weapon: social media.

Knowing she'd have to market the book without money, Cindy converted her TV fans to followers on Facebook and Twitter. Throughout the promotional campaign, Cindy found herself answering questions from people who also self-published books and wanted advice on how to build a following to promote a book online.

Cindy realized that her spark—from her days as a reporter and anchor, and now as an author and online promoter—was connecting with people in person and through social media. She turned those talents into a business: she now teaches the same skills to entrepreneurs and corporations, showing them how to use social media to launch, expand or re-brand their businesses, just as she did with her book and herself.

Cindy's success is not a happy accident. She took action by engaging with new people every day. Along the way, she discovered how to monetize the process. Her story is important to consider because when she walked out of the newsroom on her last day, Cindy had no clue what a social media strategist was. In fact, it's fair to say she didn't know what one was until she had become one a year later—and was making money at it. She never dreamed of being a small business owner, but turned into one as her career evolved.

LET THE IDEA PERCOLATE

Don't be afraid to shelve an idea and explore it later on, says Lisa Jones of Pigeon Toe (pigeontoeceramics.com) in Portland, Oregon, which sells handcrafted, heirloom-quality ceramic ware. "A challenging idea is not necessarily a failure. It often just needs time to percolate."

Fanning the Flames

Once you've discovered your spark, make a list of possible services or products you might be able to launch from it. This is big-picture time; we'll get specific later. Even if you already have a firm idea of what you want to do, this worthy exercise could come in handy when you want to expand. Ask friends and family to chime in with ideas. Nothing is too absurd or off limits. I'm not asking you to commit to executing everything on this list. Just to put a bunch of ideas on paper.

Let's say that your spark is healthy living. You've experienced a considerable weight loss and subsequently shared tips with friends on how to take it off and keep it off. Your shelves are filled with books on the topic because you've devoured everything there is to know.

Here's a short list of possible products and services that could be generated from your spark:

One-on-one weight-loss coaching

Personal training services

Group weight-loss courses at a local gym

Cooking classes on healthy meal planning

Customized diet plans sold online

Spokesperson roles for nutritional supplement or weight loss companies

Fresh-cooked meals delivered to busy professionals who want to shed pounds

Grocery shopping with or for clients to encourage healthy choices

Sponsored online video series for weight loss

Books and public speaking on healthy living

From that one spark, ten business possibilities quickly emerge and there are certainly plenty more. Create your own list from what you know to be your spark.

Do, Make, Share

In general, businesses will fall under one or more umbrellas:

➤ Service: Do something for which you are paid.

➤ Product: Make something for which you are paid.

A third business type, which is a hybrid of the two, is an information business, which is where you gather and share information for which you are paid. Ebooks and online courses fall into this category, typically created by topic experts. While you may not realize it, many people are experts in something—gluten-free cooking, raising triplets, choosing an elder-care facility, budget home décor, the list is endless—and any of these topics could launch an information business.

Other examples:

Service Businesses

consulting	pet sitting
coaching	website design
event planning	landscaping
virtual assistance	bookkeeping
copywriting	public relations

Product Businesses

food manufacturer	handbag designer
software creator	product inventor
jewelry maker	pet toy producer

These categories are not mutually exclusive. Perhaps you're a graphic designer (service) and you've created stationery sets (product) and recorded a fee-based video series on how to develop an effective visual brand (information). A personal chef can provide at-home meal prep (service), sell ready-made packaged snacks (product) and sell an ebook on how to make money doing both (information).

Service Business

At some point or another, everyone relies on the expertise of service professionals, which makes this business type very attractive. Service businesses require the least amount of start-up capital. In fact, many are launched on Facebook or via phone and email for little to nothing. No logo, business cards, website or office space required. Just a solid offering and a committed customer base.

Other advantages: portability (easy to move with you if you're often on the go), speed of launch (decide today, do tomorrow) and a growing demand for do-it-for-me options in our time-starved culture (come organize my closet, for example). Assuming you've got the spark for it, a service business is the quickest way to become your own boss.

Product Business

Gadgets, games, coin purses, clothing, cupcakes, kale chips, bibs, bracelets, scarves, software—you can market a product you've created and manufactured yourself or sell an existing product you love. Manufacturing costs can be high and turnaround time from idea to finished product may take years, depending on the category and intricacy. Inventory demands may also require serious capital.

One way to minimize some of these upfront expenses is to sell made-on-demand products. For example, if you make natural hand cream, instead of preparing hundreds of batches that must be stored until orders come in, you can offer customized, made-to-order creams with a variety of fragrances that customers order individually. A deposit paid up front by your customer covers most of your manufacturing costs.

Another option is to sell someone else's product, as many women do in the direct sales industry. Stella & Dot jewelry, Nature's Sunshine nutritional supplements, Gold Canyon candles, Thirty-One Gifts bags and Avon cosmetics are just some of the hundreds of legitimate network marketing companies that outsource their sales force. When you sign up as an independent representative, you become your own boss, while benefitting from the training, support, distribution and name recognition of a large, established entity.

HOW ARE YOU DIFFERENT?

Take a look at your product or service and know what makes it different, then use that to your advantage, says Elizabeth Chester, who owns Maddy Moo Creations (maddymoo.com), a Woodstock, Georgia–based company that allows women to design their own handbags. "Because we are custom, made-to-order-in-the-USA bags, we can get a higher price than overseas-made department store bags as long as we tout that as an advantage."

Information Business

If you're an expert in breeding dogs, potty training, increasing sales, vacation planning, landing jobs or any number of areas, including the few I mentioned earlier, you could package your knowledge into an information business.

Authenticity and commitment are keys to success in today's information business because historically this industry has had a shady reputation. The field is crowded with hucksters who pitch "make money while you sleep" and "lose weight while you eat chips and dip on the couch" schemes. We're wary of buying solutions that make claims too good to be true. The best way to negate these concerns is to deliver what you promise with no tricks or gimmicks and excellent customer service.

If I created a Women For Hire ebook or online course about job searching, I would never promise buyers that they'd have three job offers in ten days. Of course, if you were out of work and feeling desperate, you'd probably buy it. But you'd also get burned by your purchase. Yet that hasn't stopped other people from making such outrageous claims in their marketing. Don't be one of them.

Even without overpromising and underdelivering, the information business is filled with profit potential and flexibility. You are selling one item repeatedly—your knowledge. You can sell that solution, training or support as a book, ebook, audio series, virtual course, live workshop, or private and group coaching. In addition to this book, I deliver small business expertise by consulting with private clients, small groups and through large Spark & Hustle conferences.

Consider where and how your spark intersects with these business types as you drill down on what exactly your business will offer.

WHO'S YOUR WHO?

You have the basic business idea and you're envisioning exactly what you'll offer. Now who's going to buy it?

When women approach me about their business ideas, they describe their concepts in great detail. They're passionate. They see their venture as beautiful, original and unique, and, in many cases, they're right. But when I ask them one simple question—*how are you going to make money at it?*—many are like a deer in the headlights.

A good idea is gold, but fool's gold if you can't sell it. You must be able to identify who will buy your product or service. Do some research and define your future customers:

Who needs your service, product or expertise?

_____

Who (among your friends, family, associates or the general public) is already using it—if not from you, from someone else?

_____

What do these buyers have in common?

_____

The best way to get these answers is to ask for candid feedback from the people you identify as potential buyers. Ask them what they think of your idea and how much they'd pay for it. Encourage them to be bluntly honest.

Tiffany Krummins invented Ava the Elephant, a talking children's medicine dispenser. As a mom, she knew her product filled a need: getting kids to take their medicine without a fight. She could picture Ava on drugstore shelves around the country, waiting to be snatched up by parents and caregivers. What she didn't know was how much anyone would pay for it. She turned to Barbara Corcoran, the real estate mogul who stars on ABC's *Shark Tank*. Barbara's advice: Just ask. She told Tiffany to set up a table in front of a store that might carry her product and ask moms entering and leaving for feedback.

Tiffany went to a local drugstore with a rough prototype of Ava made from clay to look like the real thing. She asked parents who walked by if they'd buy it and how much they'd pay. She got candid information on pricing, prototype suggestions and demand. Ava is now sold in CVS stores nationwide.

By creating a focus group like Tiffany did, you can glean valuable insights about your product or service before you launch it. Movie studios use focus groups prior to releasing their biggest blockbusters to reduce the risk of losing money by marketing to the wrong audience. That's what you must do, too, no matter what you're selling.

eliciting feedback from strangers

Find the right people to interview. If you need opinions from moms, it's fruitless to ask an eighteen-year-old guy or a sixty-year-old man. Know who you want to target and be ready with a strong opening line to catch their attention. For example: *Would you talk to me for thirty seconds about your pet peeves with product packaging?* You're (a) letting them know this will only take thirty seconds—you're not about to keep them trapped for thirty minutes, and (b) offering them a chance to vent about what bothers them. Appear distant from the product, as though you're a hired hand conducting research. Don't offer people money or gifts for their opinion. The chance to give advice, especially in a category they care about, is enough to get some people talking.

When SPANX founder Sara Blakely started working on her idea for footless pantyhose, she didn't tell friends or family. She knew her parents were likely to say things like *If it was a good idea, don't you think it would already exist?* or *Don't risk your savings because the big guys will just swoop in and copy you if it's a success.*

Such comments are common, which is why it's not always a good idea to share your original ideas for validation. Solicit the necessary feedback to fuel your product or service development, not to question or kill an idea you're truly passionate about. Most of us should spend our time building our business idea, not defending it to naysayers.

When I started Women For Hire, people told me I was crazy to jeopardize my steady paycheck for something so risky. Others said career expos were already a dime a dozen and there was no reason to create a women-only niche. Some told me that big corporations would never support such a concept. Only two people—Peter and my mother, Sherry—told me to go for it.

If I hadn't been so determined to start my own business, I would have crumbled from the brutal feedback, because negativity can bruise any ego. And when it's *your* ego that's being crushed, it's easy to give in.

Apple founder Steve Jobs knew this, which is why at his 2005 Stanford University commencement address, he said, "Don't let the noise of others' opinions drown out your own inner voice. And most important, have the courage to follow your heart and intuition."

Feedback for the benefit of strengthening a concept is one thing, but feedback for ego validation can make you run from your dreams.

But this, too, comes with an asterisk. I meet women who will only speak in vague generalities about their proposed businesses, even as they ask for advice. They are so busy protecting their babies—worried about revealing too much—that they literally suffocate them. Yes, there are times when being tight-lipped is best. If you're inventing something that the world has never seen, by all means take precautions to protect your idea.

But in most cases, you need feedback to create a new business. Focus less on someone stealing your idea and more on getting people to care about it. Start by forming a small focus group of six to eight people to test your product or business idea. Reach out to people who might be in your target market. Let them know you want their honest opinion and think up valuable questions. Empty compliments do you no good. Some questions may include:

What do you like about this product or service?

What don't you like about it?

Is there something that could be added or removed to make it work better for you?

What is the most you'd expect to pay for it?

Who else would use it?

Where do you envision buying this product?

If you didn't buy this particular product or service, what would you buy (or what do you buy now) in its place?

Who would you recommend this product to?

Who do you think could benefit from this product?

This is vital information. If you're entering an existing field, these answers can tell you how to satisfy customers in ways your potential competitors may not. It can also tell you where your idea needs tweaking.

Let's say you've noticed a lack of child-care facilities in a neighboring area. If you're interested in starting a day-care service there, you'd want to do some research. Talk to your target market, visit the chamber of commerce, check out the competition and understand the demographics and psychographics of the area. Perhaps it's filled with retirees who don't need such a facility. In that case, you'd want to look elsewhere. But if you find a location that has plenty of child-care options, you may be in the right place: competition shows there's a market for your idea. Your challenge then becomes how to make your child-care services stand out.

Just because many people offer a service doesn't mean you can't, too, especially if you do it well. Most malls and downtowns feature competing coffee shops, banks and shoe stores. All of them can happily coexist as long as they do it right.

The same is true for a product business. Not all are created equal: someone else's failure or success may not mirror your own. Within a three-block radius of my neighborhood in New York, I've seen dozens of restaurants come and go. In one particular space, I've seen three different ones. I got to thinking that space was snake bit because nothing worked—not the burger joint, the Tex-Mex margarita bar or a Thai place. Then about a year ago, a Tuscan bistro opened featuring hardwood floors, exposed brick walls, a wood-burning pizza oven and a downstairs wine bar. Terrific menu and great prices—customers realized that the owners knew what they were doing, and the place has been hopping ever since.

Like yours, my businesses aren't exempt from competition. There's no shortage of books on small business, but you're reading this one. I've lost count of the number of conferences that serve the same audience as Spark & Hustle, yet I attract thousands of attendees every year. Women For Hire competes with a variety of recruiting services: low-cost campus events, giant job boards and niche sites, retained and contingency recruiting firms and, of course, other career fairs. None of that has prevented us from generating millions of dollars in revenue.

Know Your Competitor

The next step is to research your competition. Sticking with the child-care example, your competitors include other child-care centers, preschools, after-school programs, in-home day care and even families who leave older kids in charge of their siblings or have a relative in charge at home. I include that last option because it means some people in your target market—working families with children—don't pay for an outside solution. To win them over, you'll have to convince them to spend something.

Now take a closer look at your business idea:

Who are your competitors?

_____

_____

What specifically do they do and what benefits do they tout?

_____

_____

What do your potential customers likely value? (For example, a child-care facility must evaluate what parents value most. Is it price, convenience, early and late hours, special activities, a fancy outdoor playground, bilingual caregivers, group size, ratio of kids and adults, community awards, discounts for siblings?)

_____

_____

When comparing what people want with what's currently being offered, what must you offer to generate the results you want?

_____

_____

Once you have the list, dig deeper. Google the competition. Read everything you can about them. Ask friends and family—and their network of contacts—about experiences they may have had. Visit competitors' websites and social media pages. Set up Google Alerts to monitor mentions they receive on blogs or in the media. Where are they advertising? What are they promising? What are they talking about? What are they charging? What are their customers saying? Would you buy their product or service?

Watch Your Back

In planning stages and once you're in business, keep an eye on your competitors: you can be sure once you're up and running, they will watch you and may even try to sabotage your efforts. They'll try to appeal to your customers just as you're aiming to appeal to theirs. This is not about being scared off by all that's out there—and it's not about stealing anyone's ideas. This is about knowing the established landscape inside and out and figuring out where *you* fit in. You don't have to name competitors in your sales pitch—why risk introducing them to your prospects? But you want to know everything that your prospects know, especially if they're shopping around for a solution.

Several years into Women For Hire, another career fair company that had traditionally focused on sales positions struggled to fill its events. In a desperate attempt to win back clients, they changed the company name to Women's Job Fairs, ostensibly to create confusion and capture some of our clients. Since we keep tabs on our industry, we were ready for questions, but their plan didn't work because the recruiters who spend money with us know that our service goes much deeper than name only.

It's easy to watch what your competitors are doing in social media. What's their activity on Facebook? Do they use discount services like Groupon or LivingSocial? Are companies or people in your space using video—and might you have an opportunity to dabble in it, too? Look at the marketing copy that your most successful competitor uses: does it inspire you to make changes or tweaks to your own? Studying others will help you define your audience and carve your position in the market.

Bare-Bones Business Checklist

With simultaneous moving parts, the entrepreneurial journey can be overwhelming. For this reason, I'm including a simple checklist with some tools and resources you'll need to start. I'll discuss many of these in depth in subsequent chapters, but for now you have this list in one place:

_____ Clarify your personal motivation for success

_____ Write a one-page business plan

_____ List the products or services you'll offer

_____ Choose your business name

_____ Get a business license, if required in your area

_____ Build a website

_____ Initiate social media profiles on key platforms:
      facebook.com
      twitter.com
      tumblr.com
      linkedin.com
      googleplus.com
      pinterest.com
      instagram.com
      youtube.com

_____ Write a basic branding statement

_____ Create a logo or visual identity

_____ Print business cards

_____ Get a professional head shot and (if applicable) images
      of your products

_____ Create a specific marketing plan (which tools will you
      use and when?)

_____ Develop a sales strategy

_____ Make a Top 50 list of ideal clients or customers to pursue

_____ Produce necessary sales materials

_____ Design a simple time-tracking worksheet

_____ Think through pricing justification

_____ Determine how you'll measure results

ⅢⅢ act now ⅢⅢⅢⅢⅢⅢⅢⅢⅢⅢⅢⅢⅢⅢⅢⅢⅢⅢⅢⅢⅢⅢⅢⅢⅢⅢⅢⅢⅢⅢⅢⅢⅢⅢⅢⅢⅢ

- Once you've discovered your spark, make a list of all possible services or products you might be able to create.

- Determine if you will launch a service, product or information business.

- Use focus groups to gather valuable insights about your product or service by reaching out to your target market.

- Do market research to determine your competitors and how you'll position your offer.

||||||||||||||||||

CHAPTER THREE

ask the right questions

Now that you've done a slew of brainstorming, let's take those big-picture fantasies and boil them down. Time to define your brand, decide what you'll do for clients, figure out who will buy from you, and determine how to deliver your product or service. You'll love this part because it's where the ideas in your head start to come to life.

What Exactly Do You Do?

No matter what kind of business you have, you must be able to explain clearly and succinctly what you do. If you have difficulty explaining it, anyone you're talking to will have difficulty understanding it. We don't buy what we don't get. Nailing the business in one sentence is key.

When I started Women For Hire, my answer to "what do you do?" was simple: "I produce career expos in major cities to connect professional women with leading employers to support their career advancement and diversity initiatives." I eventually extended the answer by adding other recruiting products and services: online advertising, a magazine and customized solutions to deliver the recruiting results demanded by big companies. But my answer remains simple—and yours should, too.

When I launched Spark & Hustle to focus on small business, my response was different: "Through large events and private consulting, I help small business owners turn their passion and purpose to profit, so they can experience the fun and financial freedom of successful entrepreneurship."

Don't panic if the answer doesn't immediately roll off your tongue. It takes time to refine your sentence by revisiting words and phrases several times. But you should eventually be able to explain your business in less than ten seconds. Don't get carried away with every detail. Keep it simple.

How Will It Be Delivered?

Get more specific and consider in what format you'll deliver your product or service. Is it a service that you will perform on demand? Is it a physical product? Will you offer your product online only, or can a customer buy it in a store? Is it information you deliver in a book, video series or seminar? What will your customers get for their money? What are the benefits to the buyer?

With Spark & Hustle, I knew that *how* I packaged my offer would set me apart. For example, every Spark & Hustle event adheres to a strict "no selling from the stage" policy since countless conference goers told me how much they resented sitting through sessions with speakers *selling* their products and services instead of *sharing* their expertise. I don't offer standard blueprints for my private clients; instead, each person receives customized consulting services to meet her specific needs and leverage her most immediate opportunities. This is much more valuable than offering one-size-fits-all solutions.

Regardless of what you do, build your offer by highlighting benefits and incorporating added value to make it attractive. It'll increase your chances of a potential client choosing you rather than price-shopping for another product or service, since your offer is compelling.

This applies to every business, even those that are a dime a dozen. Take direct sales. Independent reps sell products that customers can buy from any number of distributors, and they recruit others to sell the very same stuff. Instead of competing with people by doing the exact same thing, why not spin what you deliver in a way that makes it uniquely your own? If you sell nutritional supplements, consider offering your clients a service with each purchase. You could provide a pantry makeover to rid a home of foods that derail a healthy diet. Maybe you deliver an "All-Natural Recipe of the Month" newsletter where you share your favorite dishes to complement the use of nutritional products. Perhaps you host a "Healthy Pot Luck Party" for your clients and prospects. Ideas like these set you apart from the pack and make what you offer more attractive, even when others are peddling the same stuff.

If you're an independent stylist aligned with a jewelry direct sales company, distinguish yourself with the type of parties or trunk shows you host. That's what separates the top sellers from the rest. Someone will always buy if you know how to sell, which starts with establishing an out-of-the-ordinary position for yourself or what you offer.

As you plot how to make yourself stand out, apply this direct sales mentality to determine what specifically will make people buy from you, not someone else.

What Is Your Brand?

Before you get worried that I'm asking you to come up with something complicated—something that only high-priced consultants and agencies are equipped to tackle—relax. Branding isn't brain surgery and you'll master it in no time. Consider how often you pick up a box on a store shelf because the packaging caught your eye. Or how often you've clicked on a link because you found the associated image inviting. Think of the times you've listened carefully to a commercial because of a funny or intriguing tagline.

Those elements are all part of branding. Whether you're selling products, services or information, branding provides the first and lasting impression that brings attention to you and your business. It highlights the specifics of what you offer and impacts how it is positioned and sold. It sets you apart from other options on the market.

As a new small business, your brand may first be about you, then your company and its products and services. You'll fuel your success by creating a strong personal brand and weaving it through all of your marketing efforts.

Branding extends far beyond the look of your logo and website. It encompasses a lot—most importantly how you and your product or service make people feel. You can convey this many ways: visually through colors and design; aurally through music, sound and volume; and also through texture, taste, smell, and of course, words.

YOUR BRAND FEELS RIGHT AT HOME

Your personal brand is your billboard in the space you put your stake in, says Florida business coach Deborah Shane (deborahshane.com). In other words: It's your piece of real estate. As such, Deborah recommends making your property as inviting as possible. "Think of it as putting out a nice welcome mat, ensuring that it's an engaging, warm place that people are glad they visited and look forward to coming back."

Take Facebook. At its core, Facebook is a technology company. Yet when we think of Facebook, "technology company" hardly enters the equation. We think of it as a place to hang out, connect with friends, share photos and do business. Facebook's brand transcends its product or industry category.

TOMS isn't only a shoe business; it's an experience for socially conscious customers who want to feel great about the purpose of their purchases.

This is effective branding at work, and you can flex your marketing muscle to create the same for your business.

How will you represent yours?

Branding begins with your business name. It should indicate what you offer and whom you serve. It should also be memorable and—in today's digital world—easy to "type in." The name should also be easy to find online, which means securing an available URL.

Aurea McGarry hosts personal development events. She has a name that can be difficult to spell. Using it as her domain name leaves a lot of room for error and would likely prevent prospective clients from finding her on the Web. When she worked with me to expand her business from occasional personal speaking to hosting profitable conferences, we re-branded her company name from AureaMcGarry.com to LiveYourLegacySummit.com. Simple and easy to remember. There's no ambiguity or difficulty with spelling. That's the first step in branding.

When naming your company, consider if it's easy to say and spell, simple to find online, reflects the services you provide and has the sensibility you want to convey. Plenty of people start with one name and switch to another—like Aurea did—when they discover that something doesn't work. It's not too late to make a change if you've been stuck for a while and aren't getting the results you seek.

Here's a fun branding exercise to get you going:

If your business were a color, which one would it be? Fiery red, sleek white, eco-friendly green? What one color comes to mind first—and why?

If your business had a dominant emotion, what would it be? A cupcake baker is focused on creating smiles, so it's a happy business. A massage therapist brings comfort and relieves pain, thereby infusing her brand with calm.

If your business had a theme song or anthem, what would it be and why? Bon Jovi's "It's My Life" works for the life coach who's guiding her clients out of challenging times, while Beyonce's "Single Ladies" is a great anthem for a matchmaker.

What type of outfit best reflects your business? Is it a sexy bikini, well-worn jeans, a smart little black dress, a conservative suit or something else?

Which celebrity persona does the core of your business most closely mirror? Does it have the youthful edginess of Katy Perry? Push the envelope like Lady Gaga? Let it all hang out like a Kardashian? Modern mom into holistic living like Gwyneth Paltrow?

Which place does your business most closely resemble? For example, is it the natural healing of Sedona or the hustle and bustle of New York City?

Imagine throwing a huge launch party for your brand. What décor and elements would you use to boldly reflect your brand? What's the dress code and what's on the menu? What specifically would happen at this gathering? What would each guest receive as a party favor?

In addition to brainstorming those answers, flip through the pages of your favorite magazines. Clip images that reflect you and your business. Paste or pin them on a vision board and make a list of what these pictures have in common. Browse and create Pinterest.com boards online that reflect your vision for this new business. Through these tasks, you should begin to envision your brand coming alive.

Move on now to what your clients will see: your visual brand, which includes your logo, website layout, and even your personal appearance.

While there is no particular color scheme or image that will immediately make your income soar, consistency is key. Every aspect of your visual branding should be consistent with what you're selling. If you're selling upscale web design services, make sure that your own website is consistent with what your clients will want and expect. If you're a virtual assistant, your bio should be well written, with an eye for detail.

Your brand is about you, but it's also about *them*. Everything about it should appeal to the market you plan to serve. If you serve the young, urban executive, don't invest in an image that reflects an aging company. Likewise, if your market is ultraconservative, stay away from anything racy or politically offensive. Before making assumptions about how your look will appeal to your designed demographic, test it by asking strangers whom they believe you, your logo and collateral material might attract. If the majority of responses don't mirror your desired market, you're missing the mark.

Breaking it down even further, each of these basic visual elements should provide cohesive and consistent support of your business:

- ➤ Logo and photos used on your website and social media pages
- ➤ Print materials such as business cards, sales brochures or packaging
- ➤ Fonts and language used to communicate with current and potential clients

Spark & Hustle came directly from my business philosophy. For me, it's always been about the hustle. For years, I've told other women—job-seekers, aspiring business owners, and my own staff—"To make great things happen, you gotta hustle." So it was (and is) the perfect word to describe what it takes to succeed. My orange logo reflects the brand sensibility. Bright orange symbolizes energy as powerful as the sun. An orange fruit—citrus—is fresh; it's full of vitamin C. This color is invigorating and alive.

Sara Blakely told Spark & Hustle attendees that the brand name for her footless pantyhose, SPANX, hit her one day like a lightning bolt. She changed the KS to an X because her research found that made-up words often do better for products than real words. She also discovered that K sounds make people laugh. There's thought and purpose behind the name, which should be the case for your business, too.

Who Will Buy from You?

If you assume you can sell to *everyone*, you probably won't sell to *anyone*. Determining who will buy what you're selling isn't as easy as it sounds. Let's say you sell skin cream. You've developed a potent and proven anti-aging treatment.

Everyone has skin, you reason, so everyone is a potential buyer. That's logical, but not successful business logic. Even if *everyone* wanted to buy skin cream, which is a stretch, attempting to reach them is a tall, unrealistic order. How will you get the word out to such a big market? Why would they choose your skin cream?

With a clear focus on your target market, you no longer need an enormous and unrealistic marketing plan. Instead of putting out generic information that most people will ignore, you can talk specifically to one group of people about what's important to them. Is this a low-cost skin cream destined for mass market shelves or is it an upscale product found in a dermatologist's office? Your ingredients, benefits, pricing, packaging and other related issues help

THE RIGHT FIT

The fit has to be right between you and a client, says Georgia Wolfe, owner of the Accounting Boutique (myaccountingboutique.com), a CPA firm in Duluth, Georgia. As such, she says, even though it's not easy, especially "when you're just launching your business and making money is key," it's OK to reject clients who don't meet your target profile.

determine your target market. If it's a high-end product, you'll likely reach out to dermatologists and spas in your area to pitch them on carrying your product. When you nail your target market, you shorten the distance between concept and paycheck.

To nail your target market, consider these three questions:

Who specifically wants or needs my product or service?

_____

Will they pay for it—and how much will they pay?

_____

Where are they?

_____

WHO WANTS MY PRODUCT OR SERVICE? Only Apple can tell us what we want even before we know we want it. For the rest of us, it's easier to meet an existing demand, which may involve educating our target market about how they'd benefit from our product or service. Get clear on who needs what you'll offer at the price you plan to charge.

WILL THEY PAY FOR IT? Using the skin cream example, you can't successfully market expensive skin cream to people who buy all of their toiletries at Walmart. Given your desired price point, is there alignment with your target market?

WHERE ARE THEY? The high-end skin cream buyer likely lives in an affluent area as opposed to a struggling rural town. She reads upscale beauty magazines. She visits a dermatologist. She may follow well-known beauty bloggers. She shops at boutiques and luxury department stores. Where is your customer? Where does he or she hang out?

The more intimately you know your market, the better you can anticipate its needs, deliver marketing messages to drive sales at the right time and grow your customer base and bottom line. Dive in and answer more questions.

Where do they live?

_____

Where do they work?

_____

Where do they shop?

_____

Who is in their family and how do they influence purchasing decisions?

_____

How do they spend their time?

_____

What do they talk about?

_____

What do they hope for?

_____

What are their problems?

_____

What do you know about their experiences with other companies offering a similar solution?

_____

And, two other ones, which I'm fond of asking:

What makes them tick?

_____

What ticks them off?

_____

One of my clients owns a fitness studio and wanted to expand her membership base. When I asked her to tell me about her current customers, she was surprised to discover how little she knew about them. When she took the challenge to dig in and get to know them, she discovered that the majority worked in the legal and financial-services fields and did not have children living at home.

Getting this info was easy; she included it in natural conversations before and after workouts. Armed with the right knowledge, she fine-tuned her approach by upping her marketing in the right places and abandoning the stuff that wasn't working. PTA ads, for example, hadn't produced results, and now she knew why: the vast majority of her clients don't have kids.

To solicit feedback, start by introducing yourself. "Hey there—

net promoter score

Don't shy away from asking clients and customers how likely they are to recommend your product or service to their friends and colleagues—and then act on their responses. SurePayroll president Michael Alter introduced the Spark & Hustle audience to the Net Promoter Score, a trademarked method of measuring customer loyalty developed by a consultant at Bain & Company. Instead of asking customers how happy they are with a company's products or services, the creators argue that a better method to determine customer loyalty—and, thereby, potential revenue growth—is to ask, "How likely is it that you would recommend our company to a friend or colleague?" To obtain the Net Promoter Score, customers are asked to rate their response on a 0 to 10 scale, where 10 is "extremely likely" and 0 is "not at all likely." Customers are categorized into one of three groups: Promoters (9–10 rating), Passives (7–8 rating) and Detractors (0–6 rating). The percentage of Detractors is then subtracted from the percentage of Promoters to determine the Net Promoter Score. Independent studies have found a strong connection between competitive Net Promoter Scores and competitive growth rates. While a small business, especially in the start-up phase, shouldn't get bogged down in this theory, it's a proven concept to keep in mind because it speaks to the power of testimonials. If a testimonial is a public endorsement or referral of your product or service, then the more you can cultivate such recommendations the more likely you are to grow your business.

I'm Mindy Lee, the studio owner. I wanted to introduce myself and get to know you and our fitness family a bit better. [Allow the client to respond.] I'd welcome feedback on your experience here. How does this class fit into your daily routine—what's your day like before and after class? Is there anything else we can do to better serve your needs? [Use your best judgment from there and always thank someone for his or her time.]"

Another method of soliciting background information is to include key questions on registration materials. When existing clients renew or upgrade their packages, it's easy to ask them to complete up to five simple questions to update their records.

As a small business owner, you have the advantage of talking directly to your clients. This is a big benefit over large corporations, where decision makers are often far removed from their customers. Use small and nimble to your benefit and use those interactions to give your customers exactly what they want.

WHAT DO THEY KNOW?

The big guys don't know it all, says Teresa Delfin, creator of Mountain Mama (mountain-mama.com), a line of outdoor maternity clothes for women hikers, skiers and climbers. "Don't take for granted that big companies are more competent or more professional than you are or have the best practices."

Where Will They Buy It?

Decide where customers will give you their money. Are you expecting to sell online? Will you bill clients for consulting services through PayPal or FreshBooks? Will you operate in a physical location? Will you have a mobile business, selling at such places as kiosks, craft shows and green markets?

Starting online is less expensive than opening a brick-and-mortar storefront. Geography, budget, product or service and target market will impact your decision on where to sell. Even if you start online, nothing precludes you from eventually investing in a physical location—or vice versa. Focus on what would work best for you right now.

START WHERE THE CUSTOMERS ARE

"If you're starting your business and planning to just serve your local market, you may already be putting barriers on how far you can go," says Caroline Colom Vasquez, founder of Paloma's Nest, which sells handcrafted modern heirlooms for the home and heart. In 2007, when she founded the company, named after her newborn daughter, she could have opened a retail store in Austin, Texas, where she lives. Instead, she opted to sell her wares on Etsy, at the time a new website devoted exclusively to handmade products. She got customers from all over the world. "We started out on an international platform and have been working backwards from there," she says. It wasn't until 2011 that she opened a Paloma's Nest retail store in Austin. Today online customers walk into her store and say, "I had no idea you were right around the corner."

Don't Exclude Options for Expansion

Clearly identifying a target market will help you zero in on specific marketing efforts. As you pursue those customers, you may discover new targets emerging that you hadn't considered. Remember that anti-aging skin-care product? You've become successful servicing your client base of women forty and older. Then you learn that men are picking up your product, too. A Google search reveals that men spend billions of dollars on cosmetics. *Welcome, fellas!* Those new male customers represent a possible expansion of your business. Do you have to tweak packaging to appeal to a masculine audience or is your existing offer just fine?

For the Spark & Hustle national tour, I claimed a target market of current and aspiring female small business owners. We planned the agenda and marketed the events for them. Then, men started buying tickets to join us. Even though they weren't in our target market, I am happy to have them. They were smart to join us since their businesses were geared to women. The point is to identify your target market in order to clearly define whom you want to reach—not to exclude others.

You can also expand your core audience with multiple revenue streams. Spark & Hustle events generate revenue through registration fees paid by individual participants, vendors and local sponsors, and we make money from national corporate sponsors, too. I also get paid for keynote speeches and private and small group consulting.

IT TAKES TIME

Amanda Busch owns QuatreCoeur (quatrecoeur.com), in Brooklyn, New York, providing personalized, creative bridal services. "I read somewhere that success is like being pregnant: everybody congratulates you, but nobody knows how many times you were screwed," she says. "This moment arrived when our work was featured in *Martha Stewart Weddings*."

These multiple income streams increase the ways we can serve clients, and of course they boost our bottom line. With Women For Hire, if I only sold recruiting booths at my career expos, I'd miss the opportunity to sell to companies that wanted to be featured at a higher level or in a different way, such as sponsorships, online and magazine advertising, job postings and various customized solutions. Creating those options has broadened our customer base and generated significant revenue.

Another way to create multiple revenue streams is to develop a ladder of products or services, each at different price points. For example, cosmetic surgeons offer Botox injections, more in-depth laser peels and full face-lifts—each progressively more expensive, to serve a range of budgets and preferences. A life coach offers a low-cost online course, a mid-priced group coaching call, and high-end private sessions. Your customers' needs and wallet determine how much they'll spend. This not only allows for business expansion, but also permits you to begin offering clients several options beyond the simple "Yes, I want it" or "No, I don't."

Examine your business to see how you can create multiple income streams. You may not launch with a laundry list of products or services, but as you grow, this type of expansion may be the path to boosting your bottom line.

act now

- Define your brand and determine how your product or service will be delivered.

- Be able to explain your business in just a couple of sentences.

- Determine who will buy from you and learn as much about them as you can.

- Brainstorm opportunities for multiple revenue streams.

|||||||||||||||||

CHAPTER FOUR

master the money matters

I wasn't always cheap. I love spending money. But that changed when I started my business. I began watching every dollar that went out, because I had become acutely aware of what it took to bring it in, something I never did in the corporate world. I began to say no to things my staff assumed were OK—like sending a package overnight by FedEx (pricy and the corporate way) when regular mail through the post office (cheaper and the small business way) works just fine. I tapped my inner negotiator to pay less for necessities, to haggle about price, things I had never done before. These Scrooge-like habits have served me well and they will you, too.

Your money matters if you want to build a successful—meaning profitable—business. If you're not making money, which can happen even with paying clients or customers, you're not in business. You've got an expensive hobby.

Get comfortable with your numbers, talking about money, and

acknowledging that the end result of commerce done right is cash in the bank.

I reject the notion—put forth by many so-called business experts—that it takes years for most businesses to turn a profit. Who can wait two, three or four years to get a paycheck? I couldn't—and still can't—and neither should you. A key reason you started this venture, I'm assuming, boils down to an expected financial payoff. Never lose sight of that. Watch your bottom line—it's your baby—and commit to making it reflect both your effort and the value you bring to your customers. You should be determined to make a profit from Day One.

I held my first Women For Hire career expo in 1999 at the Hammerstein Ballroom on West 34th Street in midtown Manhattan. Fifty employers paid to be there to recruit and more than a thousand women came through the doors, résumés in hand. The event grossed more than $100,000 and my margins were very impressive. In just three months, I was making money.

Just a few months earlier in my Upper West Side apartment, I had assembled an IKEA desk in a corner of my bedroom and gotten to work. My aim was to convince corporate clients to spend just over $2,000 a pop for recruiting booths at my event. It took weeks to get my first yes. I was making dozens of calls a day, every day, and working hard. I spent my evenings plotting strategy, figuring out who to reach out to the next day. I was going to make this happen. There was no way I'd allow myself to fail.

Yet dozens of employers said no for a variety of reasons: they wanted to wait and see how the first one went. They didn't have the need. They thought it was too expensive. They had a conflict with the date. I ultimately discovered I had to make ten to fifteen calls to get one yes. Do the math: ten calls for each of fifty clients is five hundred calls. And not everyone picks up the phone or responds to voice mail, which meant calling again—and again. That's a lot of dialing.

But once I landed my first employer, I felt more comfortable securing the next. Even though I'll never love selling to strangers, I got more confident about what I was doing with every call. Today, I teach clients to focus on the first paying customer, because if you can get one, you can get two. If you can get two, you can get four. If you can get four, you can get eight. And so on. I wasn't about to drown myself worrying about reaching fifty on the first day.

Your Magic Number

I'm a big believer in having a very specific goal in sight. In the business world, that goal has to be a number.

Know your numbers: how much it costs you to do business, how to find the money you need to get going, how to price so that you're positioned to make a profit, and how much you must generate to hit your desired profit. You want to *make money*.

If you're anything like me, numbers make you cringe—you'd rather leave them to someone else to figure out. That stops now. As a business owner, you must roll up your sleeves and get comfortable with numbers. If you're sure you'll never be comfortable with them, then commit now to living with the discomfort because ignoring numbers is not an option.

It's probably easy to talk about your spark, your service, your customers, or your next initiative. Become equally committed to keeping numbers top of mind—from your annual sales goal to whether you're on track for the quarter. A business owner can't ever turn her back on finances.

Rather than wasting time on long-term financial forecasting by trying to guess where your business will be three, five and ten years from now, even though you've yet to secure a single customer, focus on your immediate future: the next six to twelve months.

When I started Women For Hire, my goal was to replace the paycheck I earned in the corporate world. That was my first benchmark, my immediate and critical financial goal. Anything less and we were in trouble. Anything more and we'd celebrate with a nice dinner or a cool vacation. It wasn't long before I realized I could do much better than just get by. I could exceed the million-dollar mark, which was a gigantic leap from simply replacing my paycheck—and I jumped at the chance to ramp up my financial growth by adding more career expos in different cities and additional recruiting services.

My decision to move to a seven-figure business was a game changer, and not just because of the income. I had to work longer hours, hire additional staff, travel more and play much bigger than I had before. I quickly found that I was up to the challenge. It felt good.

But this isn't necessarily right for everyone. In fact, small can be sensational: it all depends on what you want from your business. Working alone at home, making $50,000 a year with little or no overhead, can be more profitable than a $500,000-a-year business with several employees, an office and all the overhead expenses that come with it. Don't assume you have to go for big bucks to be successful. Focus on the lifestyle choices that money can afford you and aim for the right size business that will work best for you. Bigger isn't always better.

Getting Down to Business

While there are many ways to tackle finances, I'm going to assume you're not starting a venture-backed, seven- or eight-figure business. As such, the first number to determine is how much money you'd like to make in the next twelve months. Is your goal to create a $10,000 side business? Do you want to replace your

SIZE ISN'T EVERYTHING

As a society, we have become conditioned to think that big equals success, that to really "make it" in America, your company has to be a household name. But Amy Simmons, founder of Amy's Ice Creams shops in Texas, says big isn't always best. As a child, she and her family took long drives to wherever they were going because her mom hated to fly. Amy loved experiencing the cultural diversity between the different states. "It was like going to Europe except there was one language." But as she got older, she noticed how homogenized America had become, with malls and strips with national retailers that made one city look much like another. "They were losing local flavor and color."

As a result, when she founded Amy's in Austin, Texas, in 1984, she found herself drawn to the notion of staying local. "When you're rooted in the community, you have a better sense of local values—the likes and dislikes." She thinks that every region in the country deserves to have its own local brand of ice cream, unique to that area.

She now has fifteen Amy's shops scattered around the state, and she expanded into the hamburger business with two Phil's Ice Houses, all of which together bring in more than $8.5 million a year. She employs about two hundred people, many of them high school kids whom she enjoys mentoring, with plans to offer seed money to employees who want to start their own enterprises.

continues on next page . . .

But going national à la Häagen Daz, Baskin-Robbins or Ben & Jerry's is not in the picture now or ever, Amy says. "You need to ask yourself, what is important to you? What are critical success factors of your business—and can they be done well on a large scale?"

For Amy, success means providing a positive work environment for her employees. She has one ongoing goal in selling ice cream—"to make people's day"—and a long-term one—"to be a one-hundred-year-old company." After thirty years, she's almost a third of the way there.

$40,000 salary? Perhaps you're aiming for six figures. This number represents how much money you want to personally bank in salary after all business expenses are accounted for.

I meet women who are genuinely not interested in profit, content to run their businesses as glorified hobbies just to keep busy. That's fine for them. Others want to fund a travel or shopping habit. Again, fine. Then there are women—and you may be among them—who need to make money now in order to keep a roof over their head. Where you fall is up to you, but spend some time coming up with your personal magic number. Whether it is high or low won't affect the advice you'll find in these chapters. But it should be:

REALISTIC. Nothing says you can't go from zero to a million in one year. But if you've never run a business, have no idea what you really want to do, and are starting with very little money, ground your number in that reality.

RATIONAL. Base your magic number on something tangible. Maybe it's your former salary or the amount of money you need to pay your bills and live comfortably. Maybe it's the cost of the dream vacation you're planning, your child's college tuition or the car you want.

If you're really gutsy and ambitious, add a third criteria:

A BIT OF A STRETCH. Nothing stretches you like building a business, so take this into consideration when you establish your financial goals. For example, maybe your realistic and rational number is to earn $50,000 a year because that's what you need to pay your bills. But why not add $10,000 to it—a 20 percent boost—which would bring your magic total to $60,000?

Write it down. What's your magic number?

The Hard Numbers

Let's calculate how much money you'll have to add to that magic number to achieve your financial goal. In order words, what kind of costs will you incur to generate that kind of paycheck? This is the cost of doing business—these are your expenses.

A common mistake is underestimating your costs. If this happens, even when you meet your sales goals, you'll wonder why your bank account is still shrinking. "How could I deposit $3,000 in sales and still have a negative balance?" To avoid bank-statement shock, we'll get you in the habit of planning for every dollar you'll spend to make your business successful. Typically (and unfortunately) costs are always greater than you anticipate,

---

CONSIDER YOUR TIME

In small business, long hours are often a given. Keep track of your time so you can determine what you're making per hour, says Claudia Endler of Claudia Endler Designs (claudiaendlerdesigns.com), a Los Angeles–based modern jewelry business. "It will be surprising at first, but it'll allow you to make intelligent business decisions."

so we'll plan for that, too. Make a pledge now and say it loud and proud: I won't spend a dollar unless I write it down. Then, honor it.

As you prepare for lean times in the initial stages of your launch, cut back on personal expenses. Put the brakes on shopping sprees, dining out and all nonessentials. Commit to putting the money you save into a savings account and take a close look at your must-haves to spot opportunities for savings. Call your phone company to ask about a less expensive plan. Investigate whether slightly raising the deductible on your various insurance policies could decrease your monthly premiums. Use coupons to save on groceries. In essence, scrutinize every dollar.

Make a list of everything you need to get going. Typical expenses may include a variety of high-ticket items, many of which you can do without at the start. I began in my bedroom with an existing desktop computer and fax, bought a chair and a cheap laminated desk at IKEA, had a business phone line installed and hung a whiteboard. It cost me a few hundred dollars. You might need money for:

➤ Shared office or retail space (only if working from home isn't an option)

➤ Essential supplies and equipment to perform your service

➤ Raw materials to produce your product

➤ Utilities such as phone, power and Internet connection, which you may already have in place

➤ Website development and hosting

➤ Business licenses and permits if required in your area and industry

➤ Bank fees

➤ Insurance

➤ Legal and accounting fees

➤ Membership dues for networking and professional organizations (ask for a complimentary trial period to ensure it's the right fit before investing)

➤ Entrepreneurial training such as coaching or conferences if you'd feel more confident with such support

➤ Health insurance unless you're covered elsewhere

Profit can be gobbled up with invisible incidentals. Take a bookkeeper serving small businesses in her area. She works from home on a computer system she already owns, and she has no employees. She's already a member of her local chamber of commerce and a networking group. On paper, it appears that she has no expenses and has created a pure-profit business. So why does her bank balance continue to shrink?

Let's take a closer look.

No outside office means she conducts business meetings with current and prospective clients over lunch at a local restaurant and she always picks up the tab. Each month, she spends money on gas, tolls and parking when she drives to pick up her clients' paperwork and reports. She loves to drop off a small client-retention gift—usually freshly baked cookies from a nearby pastry shop—when she makes the trip. She mails her work to her clients via Express Mail for added security, but doesn't bill them for this additional expense. When she picks up an ink cartridge for the printer, she grabs some of those roller ball pens, a cute notebook, a pack of index cards and Post-its. In no time she's gone from no expenses to quite a few, none of which are in her written budget. None of them individually is bank-busting, but together they add up to $500 a month.

Take a look at just a few of the common expenses that are easy to forget when making your budget:

- Travel expenses, including gas, tolls and parking (I used to be somewhat dismissive of this line. Now in New York, crossing the George Washington Bridge is $12, which is also how much you'll pay per hour to park in many big cities.)
- Meals or drinks with current and prospective clients
- A Starbucks a day when you opt to use their office space and Wi-Fi
- Magazine subscriptions
- Bank fees
- Postage
- Printing
- Sales tax
- Miscellaneous supplies

THE LITTLE COSTS

The Party Goddess Marley Majcher (thepartygoddess.com) was securing a slew of impressive accounts for her Los Angeles event planning business. She had big spenders with seemingly limitless budgets hiring her to put on elaborate parties. She was appearing on television and serving A-list celebrities. But at the end of the day when she looked at the bottom line, she wasn't making any money even though she was always busy. Turns out, the incidentals were eating up her profit.

So Marley began tracking her time and expenses—she refers to it as "lawyer meets diet journal"—and was shocked to discover how many expenses she hadn't even thought about. She subsequently created a way of recording every dollar spent to make sure she was profiting from each event. In a nutshell, this is it:

"A" EXPENSES: The hard costs of delivering your product or service, also known as the cost of goods sold, e.g., buying flour to produce cookies.

"B" EXPENSES: Time spent, which is tracked on paper much like a lawyer registers time and a dieter journals food intake.

"C" EXPENSES: Often overlooked expenses including those little things we hope won't show up, but always do, like purchasing samples, parking, shipping and client drinks and dinners.

"D" EXPENSES: Your fixed overhead including salaries, rent, insurance and more.

Marley argues rightly that by looking at these expenses, you'll have a better handle on your real costs, which means you'll be more apt to price accordingly to cover yourself and make a healthy profit.

How do you know if you should include an expense in your hard-numbers planning? Simple: If you wouldn't have otherwise spent the money, it's a business expense and it must be included in your budget.

When creating your first budget, you might not know the exact numbers to include. That's OK. Start by making a list of expense categories. Once you have your list, do a little window shopping, checking out the prices for bargain-basement and penthouse options. That will give you a price range and an accurate idea of what things cost. Use a number that falls in the middle.

Add up every expense—plus your personal magic number—to determine what you must generate annually. (You'll have to add 10 to 20 percent in unexpected expenses, which always show up.) The total is the amount of money you must bring in to achieve your personal financial goal. Go back and tap your inner cheapskate to challenge all of these costs without putting your business at risk.

> Is working from home or utilizing an affordable, flexible coworking space an option right now instead of getting your own office?

> Can you barter your services in exchange for Web-design or legal help to avoid those out-of-pocket expenses?

> Can you use Facebook or Tumblr as your company's Web presence rather than spending money to design and host a full-fledged website?

> Could you use PayPal or a mobile-payment option such as Intuit's GoPayment to accept credit cards instead of establishing a merchant account?

> Can you sign up for an online payroll service such as SurePayroll instead of paying an accountant to prepare and submit quarterly payments on your behalf?

> Can you meet prospective clients for coffee instead of lunch?

> Could phone calls or Skype chats replace some face-to-face meetings?

> Where can you challenge yourself to cut corners without sacrificing value?

Look for services that help small business owners simplify their start-up expenses. For a low monthly fee, eVoice or Grasshopper, virtual phone systems, offer features such as a unique local or toll free phone number, an auto attendant to answer and route calls to your cell or home phone, and more. Another great service: eFax, which cuts costs by eliminating the need for an additional phone line, a fax machine, ink and paper. With eFax you get a unique local or toll free fax number and receive all faxes by email.

I'm a fan of crowd-sourcing sites such as crowdSPRING (crowdspring.com) for unbeatable pricing on marketing tasks such as logo design, banner advertisement creation and more.

The cost-saving site Fiverr (fiverr.com) is useful for simple, seemingly offbeat tasks for which you'll pay—you guessed it—just

no storefront?
no problem

Today's technology makes it easier than ever for small business owners to sell their products or services on the go. If you sell at events, crafts fairs, green markets, kiosks or other movable venues, it's essential to accept credit cards via mobile payment solutions. Customers tend to spend more when they can pay by plastic, not cash, so you'll capture more people and ring up bigger receipts by accepting credit cards. Even the smallest business can do this inexpensively without investing in up-front fees or a costly merchant account with expensive equipment and long-term contracts. At Spark & Hustle events, many attendees plug Intuit's GoPayment card reader (gopayment.com) into their iPhone, Android or BlackBerry to sell books, candles, jewelry, cupcakes and other products. There is no setup fee and the card reader is free. Pay just a low percentage on each transaction and funds are deposited directly into your bank account. This is the same service that's used by on-the-go service providers such as plumbers who would otherwise have to wait for checks in the mail even after completing a service.

$5. I introduced Ivy Hall, cofounder of Initials Inc. to the site. She was getting ready to announce her direct sales company's annual incentive trip to a sunny resort, and she turned to Fiverr to pay someone to write her company name in beach sand. Well worth the $5.

Be tough on your budget. The more expenses you cut, the more money you'll make.

Putting on events doesn't come cheaply. At my first Spark & Hustle intensive, I paid thousands of dollars for the group to fire-walk because I felt strongly that a little razzamatazz would make the inaugural event extra special. I also know you have to spend money to make money.

That said, I'm always looking to save money whenever it makes sense. We often stay at a Hampton Inn because the chain provides complimentary breakfast, making it a better deal than a hotel where breakfast is extra. There's a free Wi-Fi and a no-cost business center, which saves quite a bit over hotels that tack on extra fees for those essentials. I rarely invest in elaborate staging or fluff that's not necessary to fulfill promises I make to my clients. I want them to remember the advice and content, not the dancers or décor that other events use to compensate for weak programming. The last thing you want to do is saddle your new business with expenses that erase profit or push it so far into the future that you never realize your goal.

On the following page is a basic generic expense list. Use your research to get a range of price options for each, then chip away at any overhead expense that isn't essential.

In the miscellaneous category, you should allow for a minimum of 10 percent of total expenses. This line covers the unexpected expenses that will no doubt come up, the ones that simply aren't on your radar today. They'll appear sooner rather than later.

expense	amount	monthly, annually or onetime	absolutely necessary? yes / no
Office Space			
Equipment			
Staff			
Networking			
Marketing (including website)			
Training (conferences, workshops and seminars)			
Travel Expenses			
Professional Fees (for attorneys and/or accountants)			
Raw Materials			
Utilities			
Shipping and Printing			
Office Supplies			
Entertainment (meals with clients)			
Taxes			
Business Licenses or Insurance			
Miscellaneous			

When you fill in the following numbers, calculate annual and onetime expenses once and monthly expenses twelve times, to get the total annual expenses.

Your Annual Expenses _____
+
Your Personal Magic Number _____
_____

= Your First-Year Gross Revenue Target _____

This is how much you'll have to generate in gross revenue annually to make your paycheck goal a reality.

(Remember the basic equation: A career coach wants to make a $50,000 salary. That's her magic number. She estimates $24,000 in expenses—about $2,000 per month—to meet this goal. That means her annual sales target is $74,000.)

One caveat to keep in mind: The cost of delivering your product or service will vary depending on the number of sales you generate. So that's a key number that will fluctuate, and affiliated numbers may have to be adjusted, too.

Pricing for Profit

Next, determine how much to charge. Very few things create as much anxiety for small business owners—especially women—as pricing. We don't like talking about money, let alone asking for it. We tend to undervalue our time and talent, which costs us money. How much can you charge without pricing yourself out of the sale, while also ensuring a healthy profit?

There are a variety of ways to come up with your numbers.

One option: How many of your products can you produce in a given week? Or how many clients can you serve in a week? Take that number and multiply it by fifty weeks. This will give you your annual product/service production capacity, assuming you plan to work fulltime. Then take the first-year gross revenue target that you just calculated (magic number + expenses) and divide that by your annual product/service production capacity. This may give you a rough product price to begin with, but only if it makes sense for your industry and your target market.

Bear with me. It's not that complicated, I swear. Here's how that formula works in two different business models:

Take a seamstress who specializes in custom drapes. If her annual sales goal, which includes her magic personal number and her expenses, is $50,000 and she can create two sets of custom drapes per week, her baseline price must be around $500 to meet her numbers. I've never bought custom drapes, but that seems fairly reasonable to me.

DON'T DEVALUE YOURSELF

Shari Alexander of Expert Message Group in Tulsa, Oklahoma (expertmessagegroup.com), which helps experts turn their message into books and speeches, says never undervalue your service. "Don't undercut your value from the get-go. If you have something unique and special to offer, then your pricing structure should appeal to customers who require something unique and special."

But what if that same seamstress makes two small throw pillows every week, not two sets of custom curtains, and she has to sell them for the same $500 each? Unless they're mink or diamond-studded and her target market is Beverly Hills matrons, I don't know who will buy her pillows at $500 a pop. In such a case, her numbers don't work and she'll have to dramatically increase capacity, rethink her product offering or alter her wish on that magic personal number.

In a service business, a résumé writer in the Midwest has an annual sales goal of $50,000. If she serves just two clients per week, her baseline price per résumé would have to be $500, which is high for a basic resume. At her existing rate of just $100 per resume, she'd have to produce ten resumes a week to meet her numbers, which may be unlikely if she's delivering a customized, time-consuming service and soliciting new clients simultaneously. So to make her sales goal a reality, she has to raise her prices or she has to alter her packages so she generates more money by providing more comprehensive services to fewer people. The $500 package for two clients per week may be possible if she's targeting mid-career professionals and offering coaching conversations along with the résumé development services. That's a more realistic value proposition, but it only works if she can fill her pipeline with prospects to meet the need of two paying clients consistently every week.

Number of products/services you can produce in one week × 50 weeks = _____ (annual product/service capacity)

_____

First year gross revenue target ÷ annual product/service production capacity = _____ (average price to consider)

_____

There's no magic bullet when determining your perfect price, but this is a place to start. From here, do some additional research to be sure your pricing will be competitive, accurately represent your brand, and provide you with a healthy profit.

Get to know the following:

1. What are people in your target market already paying for a similar existing product or service?

2. Does your target market fall into a particular socioeconomic category? How does this impact your calculations?

3. Does geography impact your pricing? Can you get what you're asking where you're currently located?

4. Does your price align with your brand promise?

With product-based businesses, it's often tempting to set prices low enough to compete with bigger companies. But it's doubtful you can survive if you're aiming for Walmart's prices, because very low prices are the basis of its business. With such a massive market share, even if Walmart only makes pennies on each item sold, the volume is so gigantic that its profits are enormous. Add its low-cost shipping, nationwide scale and massive advertising and brand awareness, and it's clear that you can't (and shouldn't try to) compete with Walmart.

WHAT WOULD YOU PAY?

Susan Zimmerman, founder of Sueb.do (suebdo.com), a Wellesley, Massachusetts–based company that sells a line of preppy clothing and accessories, says her pricing formula is simple: "I charge the price I would pay for it if I saw it in the store."

When you're a small start-up, there's little room in your budget for what the business world calls loss leaders—sales in which you lose money in order to gain a customer on other products or services. Don't undercut yourself by pricing below budget.

Service professionals also make this mistake. They devalue their service and underestimate the time it really takes to complete a project. When setting your prices, remember that the adage "you get what you pay for" is very true in the minds of your prospective clients. A price that's too low sometimes sounds alarm bells. Potential customers may walk away thinking you're either inexperienced, incompetent or a scammer.

Consider the real value of what you're selling—the tangible and intangible. A party planner isn't just selling her ability to choose a venue, select the menu, develop a music playlist, visualize the décor and welcome guests on the big day. All of that is essential, of course, but the additional value of her expertise is the stress relief, peace of mind and creativity that she offers clients who count on her to make sure everything is just right. That value must be built into her pricing model. A rate that's too low won't engender the same level of trust. A higher fee is more likely to do the trick as long as she knows her audience.

The tangible: the venue and menu that impress every guest. *The intangible*: a memorable setting unlike anything guests have ever seen, which makes the hostess feel like a million bucks, especially given her confidence knowing that an accomplished professional is handling every detail.

When Lanae Paaverud founded SocialNetworkingNanny.com, she severely underpriced her services. She's a social media concierge who helps companies maximize the benefits of Twitter and Facebook to grow their businesses—and the value of what she offered was undermined by a rate that felt too cheap. For example, she was charging under $100 to set up and launch Facebook pages for clients, which led me to wonder if she was really as good as she claimed. I urged her to raise her fees, and when she did, Lanae says she increased her client base by 500 percent. By moving away from bargain-basement pricing, she improved the quality of clients and earned their respect and business, thereby boosting her bottom line.

No matter what your prices, you must convince your customer that you're worth it. There are many ways to use price as part of your overall sales strategy.

Can you position the price of your product in contrast to potential monetary gain? Your career coaching service is $200, but by paying for it, your client will learn how to negotiate a job offer that will more than make up for this minimal investment.

This model is used by direct sales companies. You can buy a starter kit for $100 and receive training materials and product samples that are worth much more.

Another option is to price based on the penalty people might pay if they don't make this purchase. Insurance is positioned this way. Pay a small amount now to avoid the potential of a huge cost down the road. This works well for service providers: pay for these accounting services today to avoid substantial penalties from the IRS later.

You may be able to position the price of your product as reassuringly expensive. This works for products that boast big benefits and for service providers where the stakes are high. Remember that party planner? Would you trust your wedding to the cheapest photographer or the cheapest caterer? Paying more for something you really want may offer reassurance that you'll appreciate the value of what you're getting.

This was my method for one series of Spark & Hustle events.

The ticket price was $495 for a three-day program, which was higher than other multi-day conferences aimed at the same audience. I explained to prospects that others charged significantly less because they made it up with "back-of-the-room" sales. Their speakers took the stage, then delivered thinly veiled sales presentations where they asked attendees to buy whatever they were peddling at the back of the room when their allotted time was up. Every session had strings attached. But with Spark & Hustle, there would be absolutely no selling from the stage. The ticket price was the only fee an attendee would be asked to pay. Today, whether I'm promoting a program that's $50,000 or $50, I'm always ready to explain the value of what's being offered. I don't want a prospect deciding on price; I want them to make decisions on value.

Think about possibly positioning your price as inexpensive compared to its value and the potential it represents. You may also opt to make it even more affordable by offering a payment plan.

Once you have an idea of what you'd like to charge per item or service, do some market research to find out what others in your industry charge for the same product or service. Many small business consultants suggest checking out your competition and their prices, and then planting yourself somewhere firmly in the middle of the market. Not too high. Not too low.

I disagree. Their business isn't your business, and you have to do what'll work best for you and the people you'll serve. Do market research to get a solid sense of what the market will bear. For every product or service out there, you'll find a super-low (even free) option as well as an outlandishly expensive option. There's a market willing to pay both extremes, as well as endless options along the pricing spectrum. You can purchase groceries from Walmart or Whole Foods, coffee from a gas station or Starbucks, and clothes from the thrift store or Neiman Marcus. There are massage therapists charging $250 and up for their services and those charging $25. You can have a website designed for $150 or one designed for $15,000. There is a market for every price point.

THIS COULD NEVER WORK

Price it right, says Kathy Seifert, owner of Eastern Shore Psychological Services (drkathyseifert.com), which offers psychological testing and therapy. "You can't survive by charging 50 cents for a $75 service," she says. "I charged my first client 50 cents per session. That was all she could afford and I needed to build a reputation. Because of poor pricing, I had to close and start over in 1999."

That's why you must determine not just your prices, but your pricing strategy as well. Your prices reflect your business and your brand. Are you generic or brand name? Mass market or exclusive? Or are you a hybrid? You can be a consignment shop, which carries designer goods, but you're still a consignment shop with an emphasis on discounted prices on in-demand stuff, not a luxury retailer where price is no object.

Does your pricing strategy accurately reflect your brand, as well as the true value of the product or service you're selling? Make these considerations consistent because price, value and brand are intricately woven together.

Look at the proposed pricing you developed a few pages back and challenge it according to specific smart-pricing considerations.

Consider again your "who." Will your proposed pricing make sense to your prospective customers? Tiffany & Co. prices make sense for the affluent shopper, but not to a bargain hunter, which is intentional. If your pricing and your target market are a mismatch, which issue will you revisit? What must change?

Once you determine what you'll charge and to whom you will sell, focus on how many clients you'll need to reach your income goals. How many pies must you sell or how many haircuts must you give?

Is this doable? If you need forty personal training clients, each paying for weekly, one-hour sessions, in order to generate the income you want, you have a problem. These numbers would require you to train clients for forty hours a week. If you factor in the travel or in-between time necessary to make this happen, plus ample time to market your services as you build your client base, this pricing strategy forces a situation that—at least early on—is unsustainable. You'll be working around the clock and you still may not produce these results.

This doesn't mean you must abandon your financial goals. Could you charge more per session and reduce the number of sessions and clients needed each week? Could you bundle other offerings that are less time-consuming to deliver and that allow each client to buy more from you? Could you focus on group sessions in addition to individual?

Your pricing strategy must cover your hard numbers, the perceived and real value of what you're selling, your branding strategy and a reality-based plan for making the numbers work. Few things are more frustrating than staring at your numbers and feeling trapped as if you can't possibly meet such goals.

Sticky Pricing Questions

HOW DO YOU CHARGE?

This usually impacts service businesses differently than product ones. For a product business, you'll take into consideration the costs of raw materials, packaging, labor, shipping, and distribution, plus your time and talent for creating and developing this product.

For the service business, fees are more subjective, with even more options to consider. You might charge an hourly, a retainer or a project fee. While quoting an hourly fee isn't wrong in all cases, it can pose a few challenges, chief among them is that it limits your earning potential based on the maximum number of hours you can work and the maximum number of people you can serve. The other issue: hourly rates can create uneasiness for your prospects if they're unsure of how many hours it will take you to get the job done.

If a graphic designer told you it would cost $50 an hour to create your logo, you'd want to know if that was an hour-long job or a ten-hour one. If you were told it would take ten hours, you might balk at why it required that much time. But if you were quoted $500 to develop and refine the logo, you might bite, because you would understand exactly what you were committing to.

Whenever possible, consider quoting fees based on the project and desired result—not the time it takes to do it.

When we got our adorable beagle Marly, we knew we'd have to hire a dog walker. We chatted with residents in our apartment building and got the same referral and glowing remarks from several people about one particular walker. I met Mariuza, loved her energy and then asked the all-important question, "What do you charge?" Mariuza told me she gets $20 per walk, so I naturally asked if that was for an hour. "It's for as long as I think your dog needs," she replied, very coolly. Ouch.

I immediately told Peter that we weren't hiring her. "She's mean," I said. "No, she's not mean at all," he shot back. "She's doing exactly what you tell thousands of women to do!" He was right and she got the job.

Months later, as Mariuza and I became friendly, I asked why she'd bristled when I inquired about the time.

"When it rains and the dogs only want to be out for fifteen minutes, owners expect to pay me less," she said. "I still show up so I shouldn't be nickel-and-dimed because the weather is bad, especially since it's a lot more challenging to work when it pours."

She also said if she returned a pooch after forty-five minutes, people complained. These are the same people who don't offer compliments or more cash when she takes their pup out for ninety minutes, which she does routinely.

Instead, Mariuza delivers value and results. Your dog won't pee in the house if you hire her and he'll get plenty of fresh air, exercise and playtime, too—no matter how long it takes. Plus, you can trust her with keys to your front door.

You're the one who must know how much time it takes to get the job done, but your client doesn't have to be privy to those details. Sell solutions, not time worked. You'll likely earn much more and the client won't be stunned by surprise costs. Everyone wins.

DISCOUNTS AND FIRE SALES

I'm not against sales or discounting in general, but too many "buy now discounts" can train your target market to wait for your next big sale rather than pay full price. That said, you can participate in daily deal sites like Groupon, LivingSocial, Gilt, ideeli and countless others, or my "Secret Deals & Steals" on *Good Morning America* or New York's WABC, where it's possible to expose your business to a large audience to boost your bottom line. You can also create your own flash sale if you have a list or following to market to.

I worked with a gym owner whose unique selling point was the feeling of community she built within her own four walls. But with all of her competitors offering bargain-basement daily deals—significantly undercutting her long-standing pricing—she felt pressure to join them. She got new customers as a result, but they were only there to save money. They disrupted her loyal client base and they had very little intention of sticking around for the standard fees. So she eventually stopped steeply discounting and focused on more traditional marketing instead. That served her best in the long run because she was able to attract more clients who joined—and stayed—because of the value, not the rock-bottom pricing.

On the flip side, discounting has generated ample business for my makeup artist Lora Condon. She used a daily deals site to promote eyelash extensions at her New Jersey spa, which is regularly a $250 service. Even though she doesn't make as much money when offering a half-price discount, eyelash extensions must be maintained. Women who buy the initial application at the discounted rate become long-term clients who pay for maintenance services and other treatments, too. Had Lora offered a deal for a onetime service such as a facial or massage, she probably would not have built a profitable new stream of loyal customers.

Use deal sites to:

➤ Jump-start awareness of your business, brand or product. Like Lora, do this strategically by going into the daily deal with a plan to keep those customers coming back. Exceptional customer service, which may require bringing in extra hands to handle the volume, should be a priority.

➤ Get rid of product that has a shelf life. Move out items at cost and gain new fans and customers in the process.

Before getting involved with any mass-promoted deal, be sure you know the risks. Plenty of businesses have been burned because they couldn't meet the demand or their customer service was lacking. The good gesture backfires and they lose customers instead of gain them.

Of course, daily-deal sites are only one type of sale you can run. When you are planning any kind of sale, consider:

> **Giving a reason for the sale or discount.** Is it tied to a grand opening, a holiday or other special event? Finding a peg lets customers know this is an exception, not the norm.

> **Sticking to a limited time frame for the sale.** Don't be one of those businesses that offer a steep discount for "24 hours only," then continuously extend the sale over and over again. That's similar to the many merchants who ran year-long "going out of business" sales, until local governments cited them for false advertising.

> **Discounting something specific instead of all services.** Create a special package only for this promotion so you don't compromise your standard pricing over time.

Even when sales seem hard to come by, resist the urge to slash prices to get a customer, especially since there's no guarantee it'll work. Unless your strategy is to go after bargain-basement shoppers, you don't want customers who only pay rock-bottom prices. You can't afford to sell to people without making a profit. Offering additional value rather than slicing prices is a better option. Add-on services and free shipping are better options than routinely giving 50 percent off. Lowered pricing through fire sales should not be a knee-jerk reaction to slow business.

Even in the height of the recession, when many companies

were laying off, we didn't slash rates to participate in Women For Hire events. Instead, we acknowledged that budgets were tight and we offered special upgraded packages that delivered additional value and incentives at the standard price. We also introduced new, lower cost options that allowed employers to stay top of mind with candidates even if they weren't currently hiring. Those simple tweaks saved my business from becoming another casualty of the economy.

Keeping Yourself On Track

You've decided on your magic number, gotten a handle on your likely expenses, added the two to come up with your first-year sales goal, and considered a realistic and profitable pricing strategy. Now use those numbers to determine how to stay on track financially with two additional steps to get—and keep—you in the black.

BREAK IT DOWN

Divide your annual sales goal by 12 to come up with your monthly sales target, then break it down again to see what you must do each week and, depending on your business type, even each day to make your money goal a reality.

If your annual sales target (personal magic number, plus expenses) is $100,000, your monthly goal would be $8,333. If you're using a weekly goal based on working 50 weeks, your weekly goal would be $2,000, and your daily goal (assuming you work five days a week) would be $400. Obviously, there's some flexibility in this depending on your business model. If you sell fresh pies at a green market two days a week, then your weekly number is more relevant than the daily one. If the green market is only open seven months a year, then you'll either make all of your money during that time or you'll sell elsewhere for the other five months.

When you break it down into digestible—and, more importantly, measurable—bites, your $100,000 sales target doesn't look as intimidating.

TRACK YOUR PERFORMANCE DAILY

Once you know your numbers and have broken down your annual sales goal into bite-size chunks, create a simple tracking form to monitor the performance of your marketing efforts and the resulting sales. Here's a sample table that can be easily created in Excel, which can also be programmed to do the math for you. Adjust the fields based on your selling patterns and timetable.

Investing time to regularly update your actual numbers will allow you to identify at a glance whether you're meeting your fi-

date	daily sales goal	daily sales (actual)	weekly sales goal	weekly sales (to date)
2/14	$500	$417	$2500	$1376
2/15	$500	$721	$2500	$2097
2/16	$500	$509	$2500	$2606

nancial goals and adjust your marketing strategy if necessary. Should you shift marketing tactics to bring people in the door? Are you attracting prospects, but failing to close the deals? Mastering your money matters to this degree will give you clarity, confidence and, of course, cash.

Money Always Leaves a Trail

Keep track of where your clients are coming from. While some people say their clients seem to appear out of thin air, the opposite is almost always true. Keeping a running list of who your clients are, where they came from, and what they're buying does many things for you, including:

➤ Keep you in the habit of asking how your clients found or heard about you

monthly sales goal	monthly sales (to date)	yearly sales goal	yearly sales (to date)	special notes
$10,000	$5123	$120,000	$14,112	6 bring-a-friend promos redeemed
$10,000	$5844	$120,000	$14,833	13 bring-a-friend promos redeemed
$10,000	$6353	$120,000	$15,342	7 bring-a-friend promos redeemed

➤ Show you which marketing activities are most effective at attracting which customers

➤ Allow you to customize your customer outreach when introducing new products, offers or services

➤ Enable you to do more of what works and eliminate what doesn't

Consider a simple tracking form like this:

client name	what client purchased	where client came from	revenue to date
Juliet O'Connor	Spark & Hustle Chicago conference	Heard interview with Dave Ramsey	$495
Sophie Harvey	Spark & Hustle Media Mania	Saw Facebook post of another registrant	$4,995
Charlotte Zerring	Spark & Hustle Dallas conference	Dialed into Tory's free teleclass	$495

With this information, you can see which marketing efforts are generating clients and which clients are responsible for the majority of your business income.

Start-up Funding

While I talk to many women about where to find money to start their businesses, I prefer to advise them on how to start with the funds and resources they have immediately accessible to start generating revenue. It's the best way I know to succeed with a small business: bootstrapping your launch and funding your growth through sales.

If you've come up with any of the common excuses for delaying your dreams—"It's too hard to get funding," "I'm still looking for capital," "I don't have enough money"—it's time to replace negativity with determination to use whatever you have to build what you want.

I started Women For Hire with $5,000. There are two things you should know about that money:

That $5,000 was not a small blip in our savings. It was taken from our only account, which had a balance of only $7,000. Peter and I were left with just $2,000, so we had a lot riding on this business.

And I used that $5,000 as a deposit on a venue for my first career expo. There wasn't a cent left for the things most people assume they must pay for: marketing, PR, advertising, fancy equipment or software. I had to find a way to succeed without investing in extras.

Even if you don't have $5,000 to get started, don't assume you're unable to launch and succeed. Plenty of women have started with far less.

My business hero Barbara Bradley Baekgaard is a perfect example. Along with her partner, Patricia Miller, Barbara launched Vera Bradley, the iconic quilted bag business, with just $500 between the two of them. Every penny went to buying fabrics and sewing samples to trot around for sale. At my Spark & Hustle conference in Chicago, Barbara talked about cobbling together as little as it takes to get an idea off the ground, and focusing early on selling to bring in more cash. This woman knows what she's talking about because nearly thirty years later, her Vera Bradley empire is worth close to $2 billion.

Vivian Tenorio started Signature Flan without a fancy commercial kitchen. She rented an inexpensive church kitchen during off hours. Eighteen months later, she had her own space and her flan could be found in Whole Foods stores across the country.

A teacher who dreamed of starting an art program overcame a lack of funds by requiring students to bring their own supplies. I've helped women barter for printing services, networking fees, computer equipment, website and logo design, photography and much more. The key is to get going with what you have and to be resourceful to secure the must-haves that you don't.

KEEP IT BASIC

Tierra Destiny Reid founded Stylish Consignments (stylishconsignments .com), which helps women make savvy shopping choices and earn extra income by cleaning out their closets and consigning. While she wanted fancy fixtures to adorn her shop, Tierra settled for secondhand shelving and lights. "You do not need every single thing to launch your business. Start with the basics," says Tierra. "We assume certain things will make us official. I thought I absolutely had to have the professional $200 thermal printer on Day One, but using a receipt pad didn't kill me."

Take a second look at your basic expense list and challenge each line item by asking these questions:

- ➤ Do I absolutely need this?
- ➤ Can I proceed without it?
- ➤ Can I get it for free?
- ➤ Can I barter for it?
- ➤ Can I share the cost with another business owner?

Just because a business is well funded doesn't ensure its success. Look at all the restaurants that close their doors or retail establishments that go bottom up after a few months. Similarly, a lack of funds doesn't doom a business to failure. Today it's all about watching your costs and, of course, hustling.

Finding the Money You Need

In some cases, you may need funds to cover essential start-up costs. There are plenty of avenues to consider.

PERSONAL SAVINGS. I launched Women For Hire by dipping into my meager savings. I didn't incur debt, which means I paid no interest, and the profits were mine. I answered to no one but myself.

CREDIT CARDS. I don't favor this because I'm a pay-as-you-go type. That said, many women who attend Spark & Hustle say that they initially funded their businesses with credit cards, paid high interest rates and have no regrets. Better to do that, they say, than be beholden to a friend or relative. If you go this route, shop around for the best rates and make sure you're disciplined, with a solid plan on how you're going to pay off your balance. Otherwise, you may end up with a failed business—and a large debt.

FAMILY LOAN. Wouldn't it be great if we all had that rich aunt to fund our business dreams? Even in her absence, you may have family members or friends who believe in your business and are willing to loan you money. If you choose this route, draw up a written agreement, including payment terms and timeline, to be sure that all details are discussed up front and there are no false assumptions. All relationships are fragile, but money feuds among family members can be devastating.

BANK LOAN. If you have solid credit, consider a home equity, personal bank or business bank loan. Visit a business banker at your branch for details on the process. If your bank is unable to help, ask for referrals from other business owners in your area. Community banks and credit unions may be more receptive to your small business needs than a larger institution. An alternative to banks is a short-term online lender such as Kabbage.com, which collects data from you and renders a decision in minutes. If approved, cash is deposited directly to your PayPal account in record time.

PEER-TO-PEER LENDING. There are reputable peer-to-peer lending websites where, if you have near-perfect credit, individual investors may be willing to fund your idea in the form of a loan with clearly spelled out terms. Instead of a single source providing the loan, such as a bank, you wind up with dozens or more individual investors through such websites. (See Resources for links.)

CROWDFUNDING. This growing concept enables you to leverage your personal and social media connections for contributions to fund your business idea. These are not loans or investments. Individuals make small contributions because they like you or they believe in your idea. The first step is creating an official crowdfunding campaign on one of the main sites such as Indie-GoGo or Kickstarter and then developing a plan to solicit funding support, beginning with your inner circle. (Help on how to do this can be found at SparkandHustle.com/book.)

CONSIGNMENT AND PAWNSHOPS. Have some things of value lying around your house that you don't want to sell but could use as collateral for your new business? Research online pawnshops. If you're willing to unload the stuff, consider consignment or even Craigslist. That old iPod or your kids' outgrown clothing could be converted to something more useful right now.

ANGEL INVESTOR. These people have a variety of reasons for giving you money. Some are family or friends whose primary motivation is to help you rather than make a bundle for themselves. Others may like your idea and want to be in on the ground floor of a business they think will boom, but they're not interested in being involved in the day-to-day stuff. They'll invest in your idea in exchange for a small piece of the business if there's ever a payoff down the road.

how to ask for a loan from an angel investor

Research is essential here. Come up with ten reasons why this particular person is the right match for your needs. "He can easily afford it" isn't enough. That may be one reason, but the list can't stop there. Potential reasons may include:

- He has a daughter who would love my product.
- Her company has invested in similar small business ideas.
- His firm has experience with this product category.
- He has always shown an interest in my career progression.
- His wife is one of my best friends.
- She has many contacts that would be valuable partners in this endeavor.

You get the idea—come up with a long list. Then create a list of an equal number of reasons why someone would say no. Most people aren't quick to whip out their checkbook. It's easier to pass than to accept. So play devil's advocate: What are all the reasons you'd say no if you were in their shoes? Then develop smart responses to overcome each of those objections before you show up with your pitch.

VENTURE CAPITAL. In 2011, Spark & Hustle speaker Amanda Steinberg raised $2.8 million in venture capital to grow her women's financial site DailyWorth.com and launch complementary money sites. If you have a high-potential idea with a compelling hook and a confident investor pitch, you may be able to fund your idea this way, especially if it's likely to quickly generate revenue that far exceeds seven figures. Venture capitalists require shares of equity in your company as well as a hand in how it's run. This is a blessing and a curse. You lose some control, but you gain the advice and wisdom of an experienced group of business people who write a big check to back you. Of all of the methods listed here, this takes the longest, and despite your best efforts, you may never succeed in securing a backer.

Research each funding option, with a primary focus on starting with as little as possible and reinvesting the money you generate from sales to grow your business. Don't use lack of money as a crutch.

SEED MONEY ALERT

In 2011, Starbucks founder Howard Schultz announced that the coffee company would give back to the community with a $5 million grant by the Starbucks Foundation to the Opportunity Finance Network for small business grants. Starbucks has collected millions in donations—primarily through the retail sales of $5 "indivisible" wristbands. They say every $5 donation leads to about $35 in loans to small businesses—meaning that $6 million could generate as much as $42 million in loans. For information on how you might qualify for a loan in your community, go to createjobsforusa.org/.

If you made it through this chapter without throwing in the towel, congratulations. You've accomplished what so many aspiring business owners routinely avoid: thinking seriously about money and working the numbers. Keeping money matters top of mind will benefit every aspect of your planning and growth.

act now

- Know your numbers: the amount you want to make, the amount it costs you to do business, how to find the money you need to get going, and how to price so you're poised to make a profit.

- Look at your basic expense list and challenge each item.

- Determine your pricing by considering your product or service capacity per week and multiplying that by 50 weeks if you plan to work fulltime.

- Create a simple tracking form to monitor your marketing efforts and sales results.

- Explore funding options if you really need extra cash to get going.

||||||||||||||||||

embrace the power of one

It's Christmas morning. The kids have opened all their gifts and thanks to well-meaning relatives you get to put together some toys. As your children look on eagerly, you open the boxes. One has a twenty-page instruction manual, the other a single sheet. Which are you going to attempt to assemble first? Apply that same reasoning to your business plan: keep it simple. Very simple.

If you've followed the advice up until now, you've created a list of products or services you'll sell, along with a budget. You've identified a target market and thought about pricing strategy. Now put it all into a one-page business plan to guide your company's launch and growth.

If you're going after traditional financing, you'll need a lengthy, formal business plan to satisfy a bank or investor. (Ask the bank for the specific format they'll want before you start writing.) If you're bootstrapping your business like I did, get into an action mode as quickly as possible, which means keeping the planning phase brief.

In short, don't spend so much time or money creating a business plan that you end up married to it, unwilling to change course to meet the demands of your market. Plus, there's little benefit at this early stage in parsing every line, stressing every detail, ensuring that it's *just so*. Why bother attempting to forecast what will happen in Year Three when you haven't yet made it to Day—or Dollar—One?

Instead, create a simple, clear plan that gets you moving, guides your hustle and keeps you focused on specific goals. Don't skip this step. You'd never build a house, redecorate a room, plan a vacation or even shop for a special occasion without *some* kind of plan, even a basic one. Having a simple business plan will not only save you time and money, but it will expedite your results and success, too. A woman with a plan is far more effective than one who's just winging it.

Let's distill all this hard work into a simple one-pager.

Your Simple Sentence

For a segment on *ABC News Now*, I interviewed Daniel Pink about his best-selling book, *Drive*, where he recounts a conversation between playwright, congresswoman and journalist Clare Boothe Luce and President John Kennedy. She felt JFK's ambitious plans diluted his focus and ability to succeed.

"A great man is one sentence," Luce told Kennedy, giving him two very clear examples.

PRESIDENT ABRAHAM LINCOLN: "He preserved the union and freed the slaves."

PRESIDENT FRANKLIN D. ROOSEVELT: "He lifted us out of a Great Depression and helped us win a world war."

Luce's point to Kennedy was simple: What would *his* sentence be? That story resonates with me when it comes to business success. (You can watch the original *Drive* video on the importance of one sentence, as well as submissions compiled from readers around the world, at danpink.com/video.) I've lost count of the times I have heard people ramble endlessly when I ask about their business. That lack of clarity sounds alarms. If you can't clearly say what you do, people will lose interest fast.

The simplest one sentence for Spark & Hustle is this: "We help women turn passion and purpose to profit through small business success." That single sentence invites the listener to ask me how we do it, opening the door for me to talk about our conferences and consulting, as well as the work I do in the media about small business. That single sentence tells my target market— current or would-be women entrepreneurs or those who want to reach them—that I know how to help them succeed. I can use that single sentence at a networking event, on television, at a cocktail party or in a social media post. Your one sentence should be equally versatile.

Here are tips to developing your one sentence:

➤ Include touches of realism and optimism.

➤ Leave out jargon.

➤ Spell out specifically what you do and for whom.

➤ Test it on a few people. Does it leave them scratching their heads or do they get what you're talking about? Do they simply nod and mumble, or do they ask questions? You want them to be intrigued, not mystified.

➤ Nothing is set in stone. As your business evolves, your sentence can, too.

Invest time in this to make it great. Share your one sentence with me at facebook.com/tory.

Fill in the Blanks

Now that you've distilled your business into a single sentence, move on to the rest of your one-page business plan.

There are seven components:

1. **Your simple statement**: The single sentence that clearly states what you do. You may opt to elaborate here if your work is mission-driven. For example, I might add that my mission with Spark & Hustle in 2012 is to help ten thousand women double their income through small business ownership.

2. **Your why**: This is your motivation for launching your business. Why are you doing this? What's driving you? What will keep you hustling when you're disappointed, frustrated or afraid? This is on the sheet to remind you why throwing in the towel isn't an option. Are you creating a service to support families with special-needs children because you've experienced the challenges firsthand? Are you developing a jewelry line to generate awareness for a cause you care about? Are you, like I was, starting a business so you're never beholden to an employer? Whatever your why, this is the deep motivator that's put you on the small business path, and nothing will derail your mission.

3. **Your what**: What you will sell or create for your customers or clients. Include the value proposition of what you offer and why what you offer is better than the existing options. Be specific and concise.

4. **Your who**: This is the target market you'll sell to, serve or support. Create a picture of them, using all of the information you know to be true. Describe what they want, the problems they face or the solutions they seek, and explain what makes them the perfect market for you.

5. **Your how much**: Your money plan includes how much you want to make, how much it will take to run your business, and your pricing plan. This section includes your sales goals, which should take into consideration all of your expenses and your anticipated profit.

6. **Your hustle**: It all boils down to how you plan to accomplish your goal. This marketing and sales strategy should be the bulk of your business plan because it will spell out exactly what you're going to do to make your anticipated success a reality.

7. **Your measure**: How will you measure success? For me, business revenue is the best way. Remember this is not a hobby, nor is it a charitable venture. You're running a business. What are the monthly, quarterly or annual benchmarks that you'll use to determine whether or not you're on track?

This document is fluid. It's developed in pencil, not ink. You reserve the right to change and tweak as you roll up your sleeves and get to work. It should serve as a road map, keeping you focused on the essential tasks. If an action doesn't support the goals outlined, you should question whether you should be doing it. You may write a plan from the ivory tower, but you fulfill it on the battlefield. This is your chance to showcase your agility and armor as a small business owner. Feel free to ask me questions about writing your plan on my page at Facebook.com/Tory so I can support your efforts.

your mission statement

The mission statement defines the scope of your work and the impact that it can have on customers or the community you serve. While a mission statement can be just one sentence in length, it's to be used when the conversation calls for something more robust than your simple one sentence we discussed. You can feature your mission statement on your website so that visitors understand what you're all about. You can also share it with partners, collaborators and vendors. Internally the mission statement serves to focus you and your staff to ensure that you take action only on those items that are important and well suited for your organization's area of interest. If something doesn't align with your mission statement, it's probably not a great fit for the company and you should consider passing on the opportunity.

Jessica Nunez, founder of Nuñez PR Group (nunezprgroup .com), designed an easy, three-step process for crafting your mission statement based on your purpose, business and values. Answer these simple steps to create your statement:

1. What is the **purpose** of your company? In other words, why do you exist?
2. What **business** are you in? Keep it simple with one word— list your industry or product.
3. List the top three **values** or **differentiators** that make your company unique. These are benefits for the buyer. If you're a service company, you might be more likely to use values, and if you sell products, then focus on your differentiators.

The responses are the meat of your mission statement. If you have several different responses, then you may need to weigh them to identify your core differentiators. Combine the responses with a starter statement to create your mission. Use your company name, not "we" or "our" (you want to brand yourself). Some suggested starters are "X's mission is to provide . . . ," "X is committed to . . . ," "The goal of X is to . . . ," "The vision of X is to . . . ," "X is dedicated to . . ." and "X is a . . ."

Following this format will ensure that your mission statement is clear and direct. Lengthy mission statements are not effective, so keep it tight and to the point.

DON'T BE TOO SERIOUS

Small business owners expect lawyers to be stuffy and pompous, so Nina Kaufman is laid back and jokes a lot. She owns Ask the Business Lawyer (askthebusinesslawyer.com) in New York City, serving entrepreneurs and small business owners. "I hate unnecessary power trips," she says. "I love a good laugh."

DON'T DO IT ALONE

Don't underestimate the willingness of other business owners to advise you, says Valerie Riley, who runs the Riley Group (therileygroup.info), an Oklahoma City–based company that offers personal, executive and virtual assistant services. "I've had CEOs invite me to their office for a cup of coffee just to let me pick their brain," Valerie says. "There is help to be had if you just seek it."

make smart goals

One way to ensure you can turn specific goals to reality is to make every target a SMART goal, says my friend Jen Bilik, founder of KnockKnockstuff.com, which produces the best line of humorous paper products. SMART goals—Specific, Measurable, Actionable, Realistic and Timed—are easier to execute than pie-in-the-sky dreams. Execution will determine your success.

"All big goals can be broken down into SMART goals that will lead you to achieve the big goal," says Jen. "Goals that aren't SMART tend not to get done."

So true. Good intentions don't always lead to solid accomplishments. Instead of hoping you make things happen, use this simple strategy to ensure you make things happen.

For example, "Increase sales" isn't a SMART goal, but "Through online business development, identify 50 new sales prospects by [date]"; "Develop three targeted sales pitches by [date]"; "Make 50 sales calls by [date]"; and "Analyze results of calls to assess best route to customer conversion by [date]" are.

Use this formula to get SMART now.

Specific: "Make more money" is not specific. "Increase revenue by $50,000 in six months" is very specific. "Get media coverage" is not specific. "Secure a biweekly column in my local newspapers" is very specific. Get specific. Focus on something tangible not aspirational.

Measurable: How will you measure your progress on the path toward fulfilling your goal? If you want to double your annual revenue, what kind of results must you achieve each month to meet your target?

Actionable: What specific steps must you take to realize your goal? How many calls and to whom? How many events and which ones? How many blog posts and what content? If you don't know quite clearly the actions you must take, then you'll never have a fighting chance to fulfill your goals.

Realistic: The SMARTest goals are realistic for you to achieve and they're very closely related to your short- and long-term vision for your business. These aren't the pie-in-the-sky goals, which, by the way, are fine to pursue, but that's outside this SMART strategy. If your goal is to debut your first book as a *New York Times* best seller this year, but you don't have a topic, an outline, a manuscript, or even a clue about the publishing process, then it's not realistic right now. Writing the book or securing a publishing contract are probably more reasonable goals to pursue at this time.

Timed: Let's face it: no deadline usually means no action. We're conditioned to put off what we don't have to tackle right now. So if you really want to realize the SMART goals you're setting, then assign deadlines for each action step and stick to them—or else.

ⅠⅠⅠⅠⅠact nowⅠⅠⅠ

- Create a one-page business plan to guide your company's launch and growth.

- Your business plan should include your mission, your motivation behind the business, your product or service, your target market, your money plan, your marketing and sales plan, and your measurement.

- Having a simple business plan will not only save you time and money, it will expedite your results and success.

||||||||||||||||||

CHAPTER SIX

go from product to profit

I love products.

In my office, we are always thinking of ideas for a Spark & Hustle product line that makes sense. My event coordinator, Alex Hall, dreams of wearing a fanny pack at our conferences, standing in front of a lattice board selling Spark & Hustle stuff like you see at concerts, collecting $20 bills two at a time.

Like me, Alex sees products as a new revenue stream for us, but she knows that making money is secondary to offering attendees meaningful keepsakes. "Everyone asks about buying mementos. They don't want a mug or key chain with our logo, but they do want something that reminds them of our events and the women they met," says Alex. "They want something that will continue to inspire them long after the conference ends."

By the time you read this book, Alex and I may very well have nailed our Spark & Hustle products to debut at our 2012 events. Then again, maybe we won't: the truth is that neither of us have any direct experience in this area.

Correction—and confession: a few years ago I actually did try to sell a line of Women For Hire T-shirts that said, "I Love My Job" and "My Wife Brings Home the Bacon." Some were full of bling. I had thousands created.

I was so taken with my bright idea that I assumed they'd be scooped up in no time. Today, the majority of them are sitting in a storage space in Manhattan. "Stopped by the storage room," Peter says from time to time. "Your T-shirts are still there." So much for my plan to cash in on the T-shirt craze.

This is a roundabout way of saying that product manufacturing is a huge undertaking, with multiple industries and countless books, associations and consultants devoted to it. At one end, product creators can go big guns with patent protection and mass distribution. At the other extreme, they may develop something basic on their own and sell directly to consumers, forgoing all of the complicated processes.

If you're dreaming big, view this chapter as a primer to get your creative juices flowing, then seek guidance from experts who specialize in this line of work. If, however, you're determined to profit on a small, manageable scale on your own from your simple creations, such as cupcakes, jewelry, handbags, home décor, children's clothing or various related categories, you'll probably find what you need to get started right here.

Two key criteria will determine which path is right for you:

> Taking your product through the process of patenting, manufacturing and distributing can be long and pricey. There are distinct advantages to legally protecting your idea and its function and design, but don't expect overnight victory. This is a long, complicated process with enormous risk and big-time potential rewards, which you may not be willing or able to accept. If this is the case, then

selling on a small scale may be best for you. You can also start small to test the waters before opting to go big.

➤ When you're selling on a small scale, profit margins per item can be much better when you sell directly to your customer than if you opt to wholesale to retail outlets. Wholesale makes sense only if you secure large orders, since the volume compensates for the minimal margins on each piece.

Trying to get a product on retail shelves is not for the faint of heart. Most creators run into multiple roadblocks along the way: materials and manufacturers, prototypes and patents, sales and distribution can all pose problems. Be prepared: you'll find dozens of naysayers for every one person who encourages you and your idea.

But if you look at the roots of many of our favorite products—the things we've come to rely on every day—you'll find inventors who overcame countless hurdles before their ideas changed the world. Few inventors can claim overnight success. They needed thick skin to keep working when obstacles were thrown in their way. So will you.

There are many different ways to go from product to profit—from simply doing it all yourself to sourcing overseas to hiring expert help at each stage. Let me introduce you to a few successful entrepreneurs who have launched products, then I'll walk you through some thoughts to guide your own success.

It was a small annoyance, but it drove Sandy Stein crazy. She was frustrated that her keys always seemed to disappear at the bottom of her handbag. A flight attendant for thirty-four years, she was an experienced problem-solver, so she invented a gadget to make her keys easy to find in a purse.

Sandy created a prototype of her Finders Key Purse key chains (finderskeypurse.com) by reshaping a paper clip with a design on it, then sourced a factory in China to make it. (Her then-husband had worked with manufacturers in China for twenty-five years, so he helped to get her rough concept turned into a full-fledged working prototype.) When it came to sales, she enlisted an army of flight attendants to go door-to-door to boutique and shop owners, encouraging them to place orders. Today, thousands of stores and gift shops across the country have helped Sandy sell millions of key chains.

Wendy Krepak has a similar story. She wanted a wallet that offered space to keep all those loyalty cards that stores give out to customers. So she created the Card Cubby, which uses an alphabetized system to organize cards so you don't have to fumble at the register. It can now be found in a variety of stores, and it's sold at CardCubby.com.

Sari Crevin invented a product that she initially designed to save her from constantly picking up her son's sippy cup after he repeatedly—and always with a grin—threw it to the ground. It's a strap that attaches the sippy cup to the child's clothing. Now you can find it, along with her other products, including a clip that prevents pacifiers from falling to the ground, in stores like Babies"R"Us and Bed Bath & Beyond.

Ditto for Tamara Monosoff, who was being driven crazy by her eight-month-old daughter unrolling all the toilet paper and stuffing it in the toilet. She invented the TP Saver—a small plastic rod that adults can lock into place to keep toilet paper rolls intact. It's now available in nine thousand grocery stores nationwide.

All four products launched to early success because of the tenacity and determination of their creators, none of whom had any previous experience making or launching products. None of them followed one specific path. They created their own rules, only some of which mirrored tried-and-true business principles. They learned as they went, adapting to whatever new challenge or opportunity came their way.

Tamara wasn't satisfied with putting just one product on shelves. She not only went on to champion her own product via her website, mominvented.com., but she now licenses and sells other inventors' products under her Mom Invented brand, which is modeled after the *Good Housekeeping* seal of approval.

Tamara says a key mistake that many would-be inventors make is rushing to manufacture a product without first figuring out if it's already on the market or if, by putting it on the market, they'll infringe on someone else's patent.

Start by visiting the U.S. Patent and Trademark Office website at uspto.org. Just because your idea isn't on store shelves or on the Web does not mean it doesn't already have a registered patent, especially since many people who file for patents never commercialize their idea. The website will allow a basic search, but a lawyer can run—and interpret—more thorough screenings.

The next mistake inventors often make is assuming—as I did with my T-shirts—that the world desperately needs their product.

Says Tamara: "Women come to me every day and say, 'Everyone in America is going to want my product.' I say, 'No, they're not.' Doing market research is probably the most important thing you can do."

Bring Others into the Process

Validating your idea with a focus group or in an online consumer survey is the best way to get objective opinions about your product, says Jim DeBetta, who advises inventors and consumer product start-ups. "Getting feedback from your family may seem logical, but those who love you may be hesitant to give you a thumbs-down. Big corporations survey the public before launching a product."

Tamara says don't be hurt if people you survey tell you your product stinks. "When people don't like an item, it's actually a gift," she says. That feedback could save you from losing a ton of money if you went forward blindly. "They are being honest and you can learn from them."

Creating a Prototype

Once you've determined that people like your idea, that it isn't already on the market and that no one has the rights to it, it's time to create a prototype to show potential buyers.

Don't empty your bank account on a fancy prototype when a simple one may do. Remember how Sandy used a refashioned paper clip as a mock-up of her Finders Key Purse and Tiffany Krummins used a clay model for her initial Ava the Elephant prototype? SPANX's Sara Blakely simply cut the legs off a pair of control-top panty hose to expose her bare ankles and feet just as she envisioned her footless hose would do.

If you can't do it yourself, enlist a handy friend, design student or relative. Perhaps a local machine shop can help. If not, there are also specialty prototype firms that can transform an idea from the drawing board to plastic, metal or other desired materials. It's an expensive way to go, but if your product is complicated and technical, this may be the logical route. Before signing on with any firm, thoroughly check their references and examine previous prototypes.

If you use outside help to make your prototype, have everyone sign a confidentiality agreement. Intellectual property theft is very real, and such a document allows you to test your product while minimizing the risk that someone is going to rip off your idea.

Keep in mind that the do-it-yourself method should be your first choice: odds are good that your vision is best.

Take It for a Test Drive

Time to see what your target market thinks. Through consumer surveys, focus groups and even live demonstrations, gauge whether people will buy your product, how much they'd pay for it and where they would expect to buy it. (Note: this does not have to be fancy; Tiffany stood outside a drugstore with her prototype of Ava and asked shoppers what they thought of it.)

Be sure anyone whose opinions you seek doesn't feel pressured to respond in a certain way. Be anonymous: if you're asking the questions yourself, don't allude to the fact that you invented the product. Questions like "You like this, right?" won't get you the raw, unfiltered feedback you need. At this stage, untainted, completely honest consumer feedback is crucial to determine if your product has a chance for commercial success.

Another option is to march right into a distributor and ask them to take a taste. That's what Vivian Tenorio did. Worried about her future with a software company, she perfected her family recipe for flan, the caramel custard dessert, then figured out a way to make and sell it. She visited restaurants and farmers markets, where she offered tastes to shoppers, using ordinary store-bought cups to gauge interest. Once the feedback was unanimously positive, Vivian moved forward with her idea, eventually showing up at the Austin, Texas, headquarters of Whole Foods and asking a receptionist to give samples of her flan to dessert buyers there. Gutsy, yes, and it paid off: her Signature Flan landed on Whole Foods shelves.

Another Product Route

If you have created a new product but have little interest in the manufacturing, distribution and sales process, consider partnering with outfits designed to do just that. Tamara routinely fields pitches from product inventors under her Mom Invented brand. Some of them go on to become Mom Invented products. Edison Nation vets product submissions and determines commercial viability. If selected, revenue is shared equally: as the inventor, you retain 50 percent ownership while Edison Nation assumes all costs to get the product to market, for which they receive the other half.

Giving away a big chunk of your revenue may seem like a lot, but not having the headache of actually getting your product onto shelves, especially if you don't have the expertise, financing or time, can be a tremendous relief and free you to concentrate on other things.

A warning: most inventors who submit their ideas to these and other companies do not have their products produced. It's by no means a sure bet or an easy paycheck.

Lawyer Up!

If you're considering going big, take legal steps to protect your idea.

Patent law is complicated, which means you should hire an experienced patent lawyer to file your application or at least assist you in the process. Prices will vary depending on where you live, but this will cost thousands of dollars depending on the complexity of your filing.

Most inventors and product creators stress the importance of paying for the best legal counsel you can afford. Not having the right packaging is forgivable and fixable; not adequately protecting your idea legally can ruin you financially.

To find adequate legal counsel, ask other inventors for recommendations, then schedule consultations with a few firms before settling on the right one. You can also visit your local SBA (Small Business Administration) or SCORE office to speak with a counselor who can offer recommendations. If necessary, consider asking the counselor to sign a simple nondisclosure agreement

trademark and patent defined

A **trademark** is used to protect a name, symbol, word or device used for commercial purposes, and a **patent** for an invention grants a property right to the inventor that prevents another person or business from making, selling or using the invention.

before you reveal your idea to him or her. You can find an example of an NDA at SparkandHustle.com/book.

Patents can take years to secure and often involve a lot of back-and-forth with patent examiners, which requires patience. Once your patent is filed, however, your idea will be protected with a

CREATING SPA PRODUCTS

Alyssa Middleton, owner of Vintage Body Spa, which offers a wide range of paraben-free bath and body spa products, is always asked for advice on how to start a line, so she started the Bath and Body Academy (bathand bodyacademy.com) to offer an e-course on launching a beauty business. These are seven of her steps to developing a spa line:

1. **Know your ideal customer.** This will determine the kind of products you make (high-end; vegan; only natural ingredients; no sulfates, para-bens or artificial colorants), and that leads you directly to the ingredi-ents you will or won't include in the products.

2. **Consider private label to launch.** If you have no experience in creat-ing products, consider starting with products that are privately labeled, where someone else uses her or his experience, knowledge and facili-ties to make the products and package them for you, but with your own branded label on them. You can also opt for premade bases that allow you to add your own color or scents to make it your own.

3. **Do your research.** There are a number of rules and regulations the Food and Drug Administration, which oversees this industry, has cover-ing sanitation practices while you're making products, product labeling and claims you can or cannot make about what the product will do for the customer. It's also critical to research different ingredients in a for-mula, what benefit each ingredient provides, the amount to use in the formula, and any contraindications. For example, if someone has nut allergies, you don't want to use peanut or sweet almond oil in your prod-ucts designed for that person. There is a lot to learn, but there are end-less resources available to anyone willing to put in the time and effort.

4. **Start with tested formulas and make your own tweaks.** There are inexpensive ebooks and courses to learn how to make a product from scratch. Invest in learning and then tweak the formulas to make your own unique creation. Simply changing one ingredient, such as grape seed oil for olive oil, can change the overall look and feel of the finished product and may provide different benefits to the customer. You can save a lot of time and money by making a small investment up front to learn how to make a product and then to tweak existing formulas, rather than trying to create your own from scratch.

5. **Experiment.** It's pretty rare that the first attempt at making a new formula will turn out exactly right. This is why it is critical to take detailed notes and only make one change at a time to a formula. Don't substitute three new oils at one time, because if it's not just how you like it, you won't know which of the oils to change or remove. You'll also need detailed notes for when you send your final product off for safety testing, to be sure you're using the right levels of preservatives to keep mold, fungus and bacteria from growing in your products.

6. **Join a trade association.** The Indie Beauty Network (www.indiebeauty .com) is ideal for connecting with others in the industry to ask questions, learn about new legislation, get feedback on suppliers and label design and receive support and encouragement from others in the field. Indie Beauty Network also offers member discounts from some ingredient and packaging suppliers, which can save you a lot of money.

7. **Consider getting coaching from a knowledgeable source.** Use someone else's expertise to cut your learning curve. An experienced person can steer you away from starting a business with twelve products and offering each one in fifty different scents. It may seem like a good idea to someone just starting out to offer that many options, but the beginner doesn't realize the sheer volume of ingredients and scents you must have on hand at all times in such a situation, to fill any order that comes in.

patent-pending status. This is important because if your idea is good, bigger fish may want to buy your patent or compete against you if you refuse to sell it. Having solid legal advice will prove essential here, too.

Packaging Your Product

Begin the process of branding your product by creating a great name, appealing logo and eye-catching packaging so the product has a chance of standing out on retail shelves.

Inventors spend countless hours scouting potential packaging for their products since it often determines if customers will pick it up and buy it and it often justifies pricing. Consider the cosmetics industry, where similar or downright identical products are sold at various price points largely because of packaging. Inventors tour retail stores, snap pictures of packaging they like, and make notes of potential vendors—often found on the bottom of the packaging itself. You can do this as well.

That's exactly how Vivian found packaging for Signature Flan. She scoured the refrigerated shelves in supermarkets for comparable products and looked at the packaging for manufacturers' names. She contacted them to ask for container samples, always positioning herself as a potential customer who might place a sizable order if all went well. She secured enough samples to test the product for the duration and temperature that would mirror the typical shelf life from stove top to store to customer kitchen—and she went through multiple options before settling on the best bet.

Which product packaging stands out to you on store shelves? Imagine where your product is likely to be featured. Ask yourself what it would take for your product to grab a shopper's attention.

WHAT'S OUTSIDE COUNTS

"A purchasing decision is highly emotional. The color, shape, look, feel. All of this conjures up an emotion—the make or break difference between a buyer choosing your product or the one next to it," says branding expert Samantha Ettus (samanthaettus.com). "Just like when we choose our favorite presidential candidate, or which friends to spend time with or which shows to watch, it is based on how the people or products make us feel. Make sure your product appeals to all five senses. Every details counts." Samantha points to Steve Jobs as the standard bearer. "Some called him a control freak because he ran a multibillion dollar company, yet still insisted on being involved in everything having to do with how his products looked. His success justified every bit of his attention to detail."

TAKE TIME TO KNOW WHAT YOU WANT

Mica May's vision of creating what has become my favorite custom-made books took time to percolate. "When I first came up with the idea for May Books (maybooks.com), I dove headlong into the paper world," Mica says. "I practically lived at a design center, camped out with hundreds of different cover stocks. I took them home and created mock-up books with all the different samples. The moment I found my dream paper was love at first sight. The soft canvas felt delicious on my fingers. Thus began my journey of finding the perfect manufacturer for May Books that could deliver exactly what I knew I wanted."

Your packaging only has a few seconds to catch a shopper's eye, make the shopper pause, and incite a purchase. Creating dynamic packaging is worth every ounce of your attention.

YOU'VE GOT THREE SECONDS

Launching a product? Consider this: the average consumer spends just three seconds looking at packaging, then moves on, says Romy Taormina, cofounder of Psi Bands (psibands.com), a Pacific Grove, California–based company that sells drug-free acupressure wrist bands to help relieve nausea from morning and motion sickness. "Make sure to capture them in those three seconds."

Manufacture Your Product

Among the biggest manufacturing questions is where to produce your product: here or overseas? What's the minimum count a manufacturer will produce? How much money is needed for a deposit? How can you guarantee quality? What happens if the products are produced and shipped incorrectly or poorly?

MANUFACTURING MATTERS

Kathleen Parisi of Bensalem, Pennsylvania, owns Lock-A-Bye Bags (lock abye.com), which makes a tote bag with a dual locking mechanism that allows you to lock the zipper and lock the bag to any secured object. When picking a manufacturer for your product, she says to go with a pro. "Don't choose the least expensive manufacturer. Choose one that has experience in your industry and ask for samples of what they have produced."

Manufacturing, like any other aspect of business success, hinges on creating relationships. It's not a one-step process; you aren't likely to find the perfect fit for your product after the first phone call. You'll want to do thorough research—perform your due diligence—and ask for referrals from people with products you know and like. Cold-call someone whose product you admire, especially if it's another small business owner. Tamara Monosoff suggests attending a trade show where you can chat up vendors whose products are in the same genre (made of plastic or cloth, a toy, or a household item) to ask where they manufacture their products. When you talk to a manufacturer in person or on the phone, ask to speak with some of their customers. If you are not well connected in the inventor community, you can make great inroads in the group forums on LinkedIn, Edison Nation or Mom Invented.

BEFORE HIRING ANYONE . . .

Agree on a statement of work (SOW), says Kelly Foreman, founder of Mop-Top Hair (moptophair.com), products for people with curly hair. "Get an SOW from anyone you ask to work with you, even if it's a 'friend,'" Kelly says. "The agreement should cover specifics about what work you want done, how long it'll take from start to finish, any special requirements and, finally, penalties if they do not finish on the specified date."

If you're considering working with a manufacturer that you can't visit in person, ask for a Skype call so you can speak face-to-face. Be sure there are no language barriers and that you're confident the manufacturer understands your vision.

Every inventor will tell you that a manufacturer can be your best friend or your worst nightmare. Aligning with the wrong manufacturer can destroy your momentum and derail your success. Do not sign with anyone until you feel absolutely comfortable with that manufacturer's answers to every question you have posed.

AMELIA LOCK'S LOOK AT FINDING A MANUFACTURER

To find manufacturers for my Amelia Rose Designs jewelry (ameliarosede sign.com), Google is the starting point. When I find a possibility, I ask how they treat their employees, whether they are certified and up to code, and about their customer service. I ask to see samples of their work and whether they will sign a nondisclosure agreement (NDA). A good company will not release the names of other designers they work for and they're happy to sign an NDA.

If someone is willing to work with you for almost nothing, watch out: nothing is free and some things are too good to be true. Watch out for slick types who smell a newbie. I was clueless at first when it came to manufacturing, and one manufacturer took advantage of that.

I always test-drive a manufacturer with a sample.

I found one small company in upstate New York on the Web, a family-run business, and we had a few hiccups at first. They took every piece back, didn't charge me to fix them and never said, "That wasn't our fault." When I find a good manufacturer, I stick with them.

When looking for a manufacturer, consider the following:

- Ask questions. If the first person you call doesn't do what you need, ask them if they know anyone who does.

- Have samples of your vision to present to the manufacturer. You will be taken more seriously and get a better quote if someone can see what you want.

- Remember, you are doing them a favor, not the other way around. Don't shy away from demanding answers.

- Always ask your manufacturer for suggestions on ways to cut costs or manufacture in a more efficient way.

- Get multiple bids. You won't know if the price, quality or production schedule is the right fit for you until you compare multiple proposals from a variety of manufacturers. Shop around before settling.

- Negotiate. Everything from price to turnaround time is negotiable.

> ## INVENTOR BEWARE
>
> If you're an inventor, beware of firms that promise to get your product on shelves, says Melinda Knight, who owns Womentorz (womentorz.com), an online forum that supports women inventors. "Some companies that say they'll bring your invention to market are legit. But most take your money and won't get you anywhere."

Direct to Consumer

What if you have a knack for making unique jewelry, food, crafts, notebooks, clothing, accessories or some other product, but no desire to see your product mass-produced and sitting on big-box retail shelves? You can still make a hefty profit by staying small and launching your product line through home parties, green markets, craft shows and online through your own site or sites like Etsy.

The benefits of starting small and selling direct to consumers include having much lower start-up costs, fewer legal concerns, minimal financial risk and the ability to respond to clients' needs immediately.

You can conduct your viability study much less formally, too. In many cases, you can test your concept simply by creating your product and going directly to market. For example, a cafe waitress dreamed of opening a catering company. Instead of focusing on traditional parties or corporate events, she wondered if her idea for a boxed-lunch delivery service would fly in her town. She took a week off from work, printed a simple menu of lunch options along with prices and placed copies at the front desk of a dozen area businesses. Employees were instructed to email their orders by ten the next morning to guarantee lunchtime delivery. This was her test and it worked: people at more than half the businesses placed orders. That gave her the confidence to launch the company.

Breaking Through the Clutter

As with any other business, your product should have a unique selling point that sets it apart from other options. How many grueling hours you put into each batch of baked goods or each hand-beaded custom dress is important only to you. The fact that what you're offering is made by you isn't necessarily a selling factor either. So get really clear about what sets you apart and why your target market should buy your products.

Oftentimes this may come down to materials or ingredients. You can't sell "Made in America" if the majority of your parts come from overseas. You can't tout green and all-natural when your products create waste or use animal-tested ingredients. You can't set yourself apart using the easiest and cheapest if you're going for luxury status. Put careful thought into how materials impact pricing and perception.

Why are you choosing these particular materials or ingredients? How does your choice impact your customers? Will it resonate with their values? How can your picks be turned into a competitive advantage for your products?

Give Them a Sneak Peek

As a product creator, you have the opportunity to involve your customers and prospects in your business or product launch. Use social media to give your followers a sneak peek at products

PIGGYBACK A TRADE SHOW

Like so many women, Jenifer and Sarah Caplan loved the latest must-have shoe but never made it far before feeling the pain. Knowing their fashion-forward feet just couldn't take it anymore, they wanted to design a foot-saving shoe. With backgrounds in financing and public relations, the sisters' brainstorm led to the creation of Footzyrolls, the rollable shoe (footzyrolls .com).

"To land our first retail account we found a sales rep who was already doing a trade show and contacted them to see if we could get into their booth," says Sarah about the process for landing retail accounts. Since reps don't just take anyone, she and her sister "begged"—and their persistence paid off.

"We couldn't afford the risk of getting our own booth and we only had samples. We negotiated a $500 flat fee to be in their booth, plus commission on each sale. For that, we got a thirty-inch round table in their booth. Jenifer and I literally stopped anyone and everyone who walked by to explain what Footzyrolls are and to gauge interest."

The most immediate result: landing a store at Miami International Airport. The Footzyroll founders generated $15,000 in initial orders off a sample prototype at that trade show, which gave them the confidence to go full steam ahead.

Footzyrolls are now sold in more than two thousand locations worldwide. To save money, the company still shares booth space within trade shows, but with a slightly different twist, says Sarah. "We look for companies that complement our products rather than going through a multi-line sales rep."

you're working on. In fact, consider giving them a backstage pass to the entire process.

Blog about products you're working on, where they come from and what inspires you. Ask your target market to help name the product or contribute color, pattern or flavor ideas. Supercharge this sneak-peek marketing strategy by shooting a few videos of you in action working on your product.

Intimacies like this endear you to your target market, drum up interest for new products and turn your casual buyers into loyal fans. Focus on how you can begin involving your target market in your product-creation process.

A Picture's Worth...

Keep in mind—especially when you're selling online—that your potential customers can't hold, feel, smell or try on your products. You'll need compelling pictures and text to convey all of that and more. With so much riding on this, hire a professional photographer to take your product shots. If this isn't financially feasible, research online how to take proper pictures. Another option is to buy a collapsible photo studio box designed specifically for simple product shots.

Do your best to name and describe your products in a way that captures and holds your market's attention. Make a list of the product's most marketable attributes. Maybe it's your one-of-a-kind designs or the fact that your products are all fair-trade and cruelty-free. Perhaps it's a truly unique spin on an otherwise standard product. Whatever it is, be sure the copy describing your product is savvy enough to sell because it makes the reader feel connected to what you're offering.

Be creative and literal at the same time in your descriptions and use your most important information at the top. When tagging your product, especially on sites like Etsy or blogs, don't limit yourself to just your business name or product name. Instead, include the words or phrases that your market is likely to search for, like "stationery," "hand-drawn," "thank-you cards."

Explore Etsy for inspiration on photos and descriptions, and pay particular attention to bestsellers.

It's Go Time

There may very well be only one typical path to get your products on retail shelves or into the hands of your target market, but if there is, none of the women I know who've launched successful products have followed it. In fact, all of them succeeded because they continued to forge ahead despite adversity. They always remained determined to find a way, no matter what the path, to get their products into consumers' hands. Most of them admit in retrospect that they had very little idea of what to do or what to expect. They made up the rules—and broke a few—as they went along. Amen!

One of the most notable examples is Elf on the Shelf. Carol Aebersold, Chanda Bell and Christa Pitts told my Atlanta Spark & Hustle audience about pitching their original take on a timeless Christmas classic: a small doll-like Elf who watches over a household and tells Santa who's been naughty or nice, along with a companion book about the family holiday tradition. Publisher after publisher hated their idea. One said it was so bad that it was destined for the return bins before it even launched. *Nice!* Fed up with their inability to lock in a buyer, this mom/daughters trio launched the idea themselves in 2005. They had to learn the industry, deplete their savings, make personal sacrifices to put every dollar into the business, and in essence hustle to make their dream a reality. Since then, they have sold more than two million Elf on the Shelf kits, generated a sizable celebrity following and debuted a television special based on their character and story line.

If you believe strongly enough in your idea, just as these women did, rejection from others won't derail your success. It will never be an easy ride, but you can zigzag your way to victory.

ⅢⅢ act now ⅢⅢⅢⅢⅢⅢⅢⅢⅢⅢⅢⅢⅢⅢⅢⅢⅢⅢⅢⅢⅢⅢⅢⅢⅢⅢⅢⅢⅢⅢⅢⅢⅢⅢ

- Get ready for a long ride: product manufacturing is a gigantic undertaking with multiple industries and countless books, associations and consultants devoted to the process. Solicit the support and resources of experts in the industry.

- Make a prototype. You may be able to fashion a rough one yourself. If you use outside help, have everyone sign a confidentiality agreement. Conduct viability studies.

- Research manufacturers thoroughly before settling on one.

- Get clear about what sets your product apart from the pack and why your target market will buy it.

- When manufacturing your own product to sell online, remember that potential customers can't hold, feel, smell or try on your products. Take pictures and write descriptions to convey all of that and more.

- Create your own rules to bring your product to life.

||||||||||||||||||

market with muscle

There are two ways to market your business: with money or with muscle. You can spend a fortune on marketing with no guaranteed results or stretch your muscles to reach your target market and convince them to believe in you and what you're offering.

Even if you have the money to let somebody else do it for you, I believe strongly in handling your own marketing: it keeps your eyes on the prize—attracting attention—and helps you focus. Besides, who knows your business better than you? Why leave this key aspect to someone else?

MAKE A DIFFERENCE

Bonnie Ross-Parker, owner of Joy of Connecting in Smyrna, Georgia (the joyofconnecting.com), a customer acquisition and marketing program for women who want to grow their business, says she has three keys to success: "Do what others don't. Leave positive imprints everywhere you go and in everything you do. Make a difference in people's lives."

Marketing has a two-pronged purpose: Get your target market's attention and get them to want more information about what you have to offer. Marketing is all about getting the right customers into your tent. Selling is what happens once they're inside.

But don't assume it's all about getting your name out there. Instead, recognize that marketing is really about bringing prospects in to where you are, which may be your website, email list, Facebook page, storefront, open house or phone line.

When this is done correctly, you'll reach the right people, get them interested in what you have to offer, then move in for the sale. Sometimes the sale will happen naturally, without involvement from you, because the marketing efforts worked like a charm. For example, my office doesn't speak to everyone who registers for a Spark & Hustle event. The vast majority of attendees register online after responding to marketing tactics that convinced them to visit our website. They saw what they liked and signed up to join us.

Your Attention, Please

Every day, we face a barrage of commercials on TV and radio, pop-up ads on the Web, viral videos, billboards and experts on a variety of news and entertainment programs who push their brand while sharing their expertise. We are so inundated by marketing messages that we've become good at dodging them. We routinely click that remote during commercials, hit the X to close pop-ups and opt out of spam emails.

That means getting your market to listen is a challenge, but not an insurmountable one.

BE REAL

Never lie. Even the fanciest container can't hide its contents for-ever. When customers sense that something's not quite right with your message, especially if it screams of over-promising, you'll lose them. They don't have to put up with it for one simple reason: there are many other places to go. As such, be straight. Hype is fine, as long as you stay real. I can tout why I believe Spark & Hustle events are the best conferences for small business owners, but if attendees leave disappointed time and again, my message will soon be challenged—loudly and angrily. If I promise specific benefits, I must deliver on them. That applies to you, too.

BE ORIGINAL

This doesn't mean you have to reinvent the wheel. Career fairs are a dime a dozen, but with Women For Hire, I put my spin on it by focusing specifically on women. There's no shortage of coffee shops, but each can tout a unique ambiance. Life coaches pop up by the second, but those with a distinct voice cut through the clut-ter. Since there are likely so many other options in your field, fig-ure out how you stand out.

BE SOLICITOUS

Super Bowl Sunday is the only day when we're all eager to watch TV commercials. The Doritos ad campaign—funny, outrageous spots from the chip lovers themselves—are among the best. These fan-generated spots stand out from many of the glossy, over-the-top, graphics-heavy commercials produced by top-notch, award-winning global ad agencies. Viewers are excited about seeing real people go for it on national TV. For a different investment, Doritos gets a series of creative, original ads that break through the clutter on game day. Take a page from that success: You have funny and creative friends and family. Reach out to them for marketing ideas. Cast an even wider net on your Facebook page or through local media channels. You may be surprised by some of the submissions you receive.

For Spark & Hustle, we ran a contest inviting current and closeted graphic designers to create a full-page magazine ad to generate registrations for the twenty-city tour. The prize: the winning ad would appear in *SUCCESS* magazine and the designer would receive $500. Not only did we meet our need of having an ad to run, but we generated even more buzz about our events by involving the entire community. Just the contest itself generated sales long before the ad ran.

BE SMART

Once you've grabbed your market's attention, make sure your message is infused with content that makes people want to know more. That goes for everything from your website to your Twitter background to your speaking engagements to your business card to your email signature. Consider every interaction with your target market as an opportunity to make your mark.

For example, in the email signature of every Women For Hire staffer, in addition to name, title, phone and website, we also have a line that says, "Selected as a Top 10 career website for women by *Forbes*." We alter it depending on what we're promoting. For example, it may say, "Get our free enewsletter with great career advice by subscribing here." This helps us grow our email list. Or "Register now to attend six Spring Women For Hire Expos."

Your messaging will change depending on what's most important at any given time. Switching it up keeps things fresh, which is another must in a crowded marketplace where everyone has seen it all. Use your email signature to convey essential contact information, as well as one key branding message.

FOLLOW CURRENT EVENTS

For bubble2boardroom.com founder Dani Tickin Koplick, creating and marketing socially responsible career events starts with knowing what's going on in the world, which is why she begins each day by reading three newspapers. As she read about the difficulty that U.S. veterans are having returning from war to workplace, Dani realized they face many of the same issues as the campus crowd that she normally serves. Both have been living in so-called bubbles—although vastly different—and have similar challenges. "Pay attention and understand what's going on in the world so you're able to connect the dots." Following her own advice, Dani reached out to the White House, where First Lady Michelle Obama has made helping military families her priority, to inform the federal government about her programs so they could steer vets her way.

Muscle-marketing ideas are endless. Think about promoting your business to your desired target market without spending money.

1. Market by email. My companies use Constant Contact's suite of products for this.

2. Establish profitable collaborations and promotional partnerships. Think about complementary businesses that would promote your services if you promote theirs. Consider joint ventures, too.

3. Blog or share content on someone else's site, especially influencers in your space.

4. Put collateral in a complementary store near yours or on their website or social media pages for a giveaway. Seek permission first; nobody likes a spammer.

5. Speak at an event and offer solid content, which allows you to build credibility and awareness of your business.

6. Write expert articles to share with other websites.

7. Host a free teleclass where anyone can dial into a toll-free number to hear your advice for twenty minutes. You can hear my recorded examples on SparkandHustle.com.

8. Organize an after-hours party at a store that's willing to support you. A makeup artist could do mini-makeovers for shoppers at a bridal boutique so brides-to-be can look glamorous while trying on gowns and experience the talent of a makeup artist for her wedding day.

9. Get involved in community service that's relevant to your business.

10. Teach a free class surrounding your expertise (candle making or organizational skills, for example) at a community center if they're willing to promote it. You can also do this in other venues. Offer a jewelry design course in a clothing store.

11. Interview relevant businesspeople and share the interviews on your site and others. The people you interview will be eager to share the interview with their lists, too. And you look good having that affiliation.

12. Create a limited-edition product or service offering where a portion of proceeds supports a charity, especially if the charity is willing to promote it.

13. Build a website to promote and sell your product or service, with frequently updated content to serve your audience.

14. Cultivate a loyal inner circle of fans or clients who will spread the word and recommend your offerings to others.

15. Pitch relevant and intriguing stories about your business to the media.

16. Reward fans and followers monthly with a contest. If you do it at the same time every month, people will begin to catch on and check back at that time to participate.

17. Ask a satisfied customer for referrals.

18. Write an ebook available for free download.

19. Give samples or materials in goody bags at events where your prospects will be in attendance.

20. Share booth space at an event to allow attendees to engage with your brand.

Oh No, You Didn't!

Marketing mistakes cost money in wasted time, lost sales and missed opportunity. Save yourself by understanding some of the most avoidable ones up front.

IT'S NOT FOR EVERYONE

At my Chicago Spark & Hustle conference Bridget Brennan, author of *Why She Buys*, emphasized the importance of knowing the buying habits of your niche. A male executive doesn't buy like a new mom. A teen doesn't make decisions like a retiree. This reinforces a key tenet of marketing: when you talk to everyone, you get the attention of no one. Profitable marketing hinges on your ability to connect to a specific market and to know that market intimately. That's why nailing your "who" is a critical early step.

TOO MUCH TOO SOON

Marketing is about grabbing the attention of your target market and getting into conversation with them. It is not about overwhelming them with so much information that you leave them confused and feeling pressured. Clobbering prospects with the hard sell doesn't work.

ONE THING AT A TIME

In roulette, if you put all of your money on 13 and don't hit when the wheel stops spinning, you're out of luck. Don't take similar gambles with your business. Instead, spread your bets by using a variety of methods to reach your target market.

Remember Tierra Destiny Reid? To ensure that her boutique, Stylish Consignments in Atlanta, continues to grow, she talks about her merchandise every day on Facebook, hosts after-hours events for her customers where she brings in special speakers, plans mutually-beneficial partnerships with local merchants and rolls out bring-a-friend programs. She also aligns herself with a nonprofit organization that provides clothing for underserved women, resulting in impressive media coverage for her shop. She reaches out to her target market—stylish women on a strict budget who shop consignment in her area—in a variety of ways, all at the same time. It works. Don't limit your business with a one-thing-at-a-time mentality. If you're after big results, your business demands big action.

KNOW WHAT'S REALLY FOR SALE

Vera Bradley cofounder Barbara Bradley Baekgaard, one of the most likeable people I know, never forgets the business advice her father gave her: sell yourself first, your company second and your product third. Too often women dive into a product demonstration or discussion, almost before they introduce themselves. The truth is that we buy from people we know, like and trust. Make a

how to "connect" at a networking event

First, be approachable and personable. When you offer a big smile and a handshake, you set the tone for a brief conversation. Announce yourself by first and last name and ask for the other person's name. If you repeat it, there's a better chance of remembering it. (She says her name is Julie. Your reaction is to say, "Good to meet you, Julie.") Launching into an instant pitch is a turnoff. Instead, read the body language and take cues from those you're hoping to woo. This may require chatting briefly about the event and any shared connection to the host. Once you have a nice rapport going—even as little as a minute or two into the conversation—it may be safe to begin sharing a bit about what you do and your business. If you're genuinely interested in staying in touch, ask for a business card to follow up after the event.

personal connection first, then move on to your company and product.

Cause Marketing

Studies confirm that the vast majority of consumers will switch to a new brand—or stay loyal to one—if it's associated with a cause they care about. Aligning your business with one that resonates with your target market can drive sales.

Pet photographer Melissa McDaniel published her best dog photos in a beautiful coffee table book. In addition to selling through friends, family and social media connections, she partnered with a pet foundation. She offered them 30 percent of all sales, in exchange for promotion of her book to dog lovers around the country. It was a win for everyone: the foundation made money with minimal effort and Melissa moved books and generated awareness of her work. Giving up a portion of her proceeds to reach a highly targeted, like-minded audience was well worth it. To date, she's donated more than $10,000 to her favorite pet charities from the sale of her beautiful books.

Melissa's story is an example of successful cause marketing. You, too, can align your business with a nonprofit by volunteering, hosting a fund-raiser or by donating a portion of your profits. This works best when you have the support of a group that's willing to provide promotional support for your business.

Ben & Jerry's Ice Cream ran a campaign in their home state of Vermont to support gay marriage. They renamed their famous "Chubby Hubby" ice cream to "Hubby Hubby" for a month to raise awareness. The campaign reached more than 429 million people in just thirty days, generating extensive national media coverage for the cause. It also benefitted the company, resulting in a spike in sales from people who support gay marriage.

Laurie Baggett was the first person to respond to my Facebook post looking for people willing to start local job clubs. After her husband lost his position, she understood firsthand the toll unemployment takes on families when someone is out of work. She volunteered to help people throughout her community to get hired. Word spread, and soon everyone in Chesapeake, Virginia, knew Laurie's name. Even the mayor sought the opportunity to congratulate her on this selfless service. Laurie's efforts became the subject of a *Good Morning America* segment on the power of job clubs. That spawned local TV and newspaper coverage of this local gal gone good. While she didn't get paid to launch this effort, something bigger happened. Laurie's reputation as the go-to person to make things happen soared. Soon small business owners sought her magic touch to help put their establishments on the map. Now she has a thriving business consulting medical professionals and others on how to develop a similar local hero status in their area of expertise.

Consultants and coaches can drive awareness of their business by developing a similar project, which can be anything that marries their expertise with a community's needs. A career strategist can start a job club for the unemployed. A website designer can host basic, design-your-own website workshops for business owners. A restaurant owner can develop a food drive to serve the homeless. This invites local media coverage and generates goodwill that can be leveraged for sales.

Website Wonders

With the popularity of sites like WordPress.com, Tumblr.com and Intuit.com, you can secure a domain name immediately, create a template website and be up and running within hours.

If you don't have time to learn the ropes of basic Web design, there's no shortage of people who will design a custom site that accurately reflects you and your business for a reasonable price. Start by asking people you know for recommendations, and if you come up empty, try me at Facebook.com/Tory. Tell me your needs and budget and I'll suggest professionals to consider.

Two cautions: Register your domain name yourself so it's in your control. Since you must regularly update your website as your business grows, insist that yours is designed to allow you to make those changes yourself. If you're beholden to a Web designer to update every word or add new content, it'll cost you a fortune, plus extreme aggravation as you wait for it to get done.

WHAT'S IN A NAME?

The first thing your website needs is a domain name. That means a URL that looks like this—www.yourdomain.com—rather than like this—www.wordpress.yourdomain.com. It must be simple to spell and translate easily from hearing to typing. If your business name is hard to spell, don't choose it as your domain name. If people can't find your website, what's the use of having one at all?

YOU TALKING TO ME?

Your website must clearly and concisely state what you do and for whom. When a member of your target market lands on your site, she should feel right at home. If customers are confused about what you offer or who you serve, they'll click away in a flash.

Clear. Concise. Compelling. This applies to the language on your site, as well as the graphics and images. It comes back to knowing who your target market is and how to talk to them. If you're aiming for young entrepreneurs, featuring pictures of buttoned-down executives on your site is counterproductive. If you're targeting a professional group such as doctors or lawyers, don't use immature or kid-friendly designs no matter how much you love them.

A friend of mine is a therapist, who completely missed the mark with her website. It was very feminine—girly colors, flowery script and very long copy. Beautiful, except her target market is men. Once she gave it a masculine makeover, her client base responded: men no longer felt like they had just walked into a ladies' room. Instead, they were right where they belonged.

Let's Keep in Touch

Marketing is a process. Unless they're shopping for a low-cost or superhot item, people rarely buy from a site the first time they visit. They'll likely come back a few times and maybe even ask a question before buying. Repeated exposure to your brand ultimately leads to the sale.

Thousands of women read my newsletters. I started sending emails years ago to encourage women to attend my free Women

For Hire events—and I still do today. Most of the time, I don't ask subscribers to buy anything. Yet when it came time to introduce Spark & Hustle, I began touting the benefits of registering for a fee-based conference. Because we had been in regular contact for many years, they already liked me and saw the value in what I offered, so many readers were very willing to become paying clients. Dozens of women had subscribed to my list for more than five years before they ever spent money with me. Had I dismissed them after a short time because they weren't buying, neither of us would have had the opportunity to work together. Keeping in contact is an ongoing process with potential reward for both sides when the moment is right.

On every page of your website, incorporate an option for email signups to capture the addresses of site visitors. Everyone starts with one email address in her business database. Build your own list instead of buying one from a third party.

Don't use a personal email provider, such as AOL or Gmail, to send information to your list. It isn't nearly as professional as a formal email service provider.

For years I've used and recommended ConstantContact.com, a specialized Web service geared to small business owners. It keeps your email contacts legal by requiring that subscribers are permission-based—meaning they've opted into your list because they want to hear from you. If, at any time, subscribers decide they're no longer interested, they can unsubscribe on their own from your electronic newsletters. Constant Contact offers templates and simple how-to tutorials and best practices, regardless of your skill level.

You've Got Mail

It's not as simple as sending out emails: the recipients must open, read and respond to them to make the process worthwhile.

Snappy subject lines

If the subject line doesn't grab someone's attention, she or he will delete the email. Your targeted recipient will never see all the great content you've created because your email is already in the trash. Short, catchy phrases are best, but it's even better to test your subject lines. Constant Contact allows you to send out a newsletter with two different headlines to test which one has a higher open rate. Google the list of one hundred words to avoid because they trigger spam filters. They're not the obvious choices like *Viagra* and *sex*; the list includes words that you may be tempted to use: *free, act now, satisfaction guaranteed, money, serious cash,* and even *work from home*. Avoid these words and phrases even when you're tempted to use them.

Make it from you

People are more willing to open an email from a person than from a business. Gone are the days when small businesses have to try to appear bigger than they are. Be yourself. Newsletters from "Tory Johnson" are opened more frequently than those from "Women For Hire" or "Spark & Hustle."

Top-heavy

Put your best content at the top of your newsletter. Catch your readers early and they will keep reading as long as you offer them useful, informative content that they consider valuable.

Make it a conversation

Don't preach and don't sell excessively. Engage your readers by asking questions and offering feedback. Share their successes in your newsletters. Make them part of the exchange.

Include relevant content

You can include original content created by you, as well as links to articles and posts from popular blogs and authoritative websites in your industry. Offer more than "buy now" messages. For example, a jewelry designer can offer her assessment of the stars' red carpet looks after a popular awards shows. A real estate agent can offer content on how to maintain home values and how to winterize to reduce heating costs. It builds credibility and loyalty with your audience, especially since you're not focused exclusively on selling all the time, which people tire of quickly.

Be dependable

Send your newsletter on a regular schedule. People will learn to expect it and look for it if you do it well. They may even reach out to you if they've missed an issue. That's a sign that you're doing something right.

Be patient

Your newsletter won't produce results overnight. It will take time to build your list to get readers to respond to what you offer. Stay consistent and creative since you're in this for the long haul.

Teleclasses Serve and Sell

Teleclasses, phone-based seminars, and webinars, web-based seminars, are phenomenal free ways to market your products, services, brand or message. It may be how you came to know me. I've offered teleclasses to my email subscribers and social media followers for years. But it wasn't until about three years ago that I realized the income potential.

I had just announced that I planned to host my very first three-day Spark & Hustle retreat in Dallas. I decided to host a free (free for me to offer and free for anyone to dial-in to listen) teleseminar to drum up interest in the program. I promoted it a week in advance—twice to my email database and three times each on Facebook, Twitter and LinkedIn. Some women shared the invitation with friends and followers.

During the twenty-minute call, I gave some of my best small business advice. I spoke quickly, covered material that I knew would interest many listeners and mentioned just once that I'd be hosting an upcoming retreat in Dallas.

More than five hundred women phoned in to the class and about thirty of them asked for additional information on the retreat. Within twenty-four hours, four women paid the $4,995 fee to register. Two days later, two more women signed up.

That one twenty-minute call generated $29,970 in revenue—and I didn't have to leave home or spend a dollar on advertising.

You can accomplish the same results for your business.

One week prior to the call, announce your teleclass by email to your subscriber list and include details on the specific topics you'll cover. Share the invitation on Facebook, Twitter and LinkedIn. Ask ten people (not four, not seven—go for ten) to promote the call to their email subscribers, as well. A short lead time—about one week—is better than announcing your call too far in advance. This way people are excited and don't forget.

To receive the dial-in number, ask each person to send an email to a designated address such as rsvp@yourwebsite.com. This allows you to gauge in real time how many people are interested, capture names and email addresses of those who want to call in, and provide an automated response with the dial-in number and participant passcode. That is one less detail for you to manage manually. (I use FreeConferencing.com.)

Ignore the standard hour-long teleclass format and go for one that requires a shorter time commitment from your guests. Since I'm trained to jam a lot of information into three-minute TV segments, I can pack quite a punch in a twenty-minute call, which is my preferred call length. You'll get better attendance and stronger results if you respect everyone's time.

Give your best content on the call. Hold nothing back. Never be afraid that you're giving too much. When you give away your best content—in a speech, consultation or teleclass—most people won't walk away thinking, "Great! I'll never need that woman again." Instead, they're impressed by your expertise, intrigued by the depth of your knowledge, and they think, "If that's what she's giving away for free, imagine how great her paid content or consulting must be." That leads prospects to buy from you or hire you.

Assume for a moment that you're attending a teleclass presented by an attorney, detailing the specific steps to safeguarding assets for your loved ones through estate planning. If the lawyer offers her very best advice, she isn't worried that everyone will hang up assuming they can do it themselves. She knows that she's likely to generate new clients because they're impressed by her expertise and her willingness to share it in layman's terms.

By wowing prospects, she earns their trust and ultimately their business.

This works for a product business, too. If you sell accessories for fashion lovers, your complimentary teleclass may focus on the hottest style trends for the season. Women dial in to hear your ten top tips on how to update their look to be on-trend without breaking the budget. As a thank-you for participating, you can offer a limited-time discount to shop your new collection or you can invite listeners to contact you for a personal showing.

Finally, never view, present or execute teleclasses as sales presentations. This is a service that keeps you connected to your audience. With mine, I offer a very brief introduction and then get down to business quickly. My introduction includes a reference to something happening today so it's clear to listeners that they're on a live call, not something that was prerecorded months ago. For example, "Hey everyone, it's Tory Johnson. Thanks so much for dialing in this afternoon. Not sure about where you are, but it's a pretty miserable day weather-wise here in New York City, which is why I'm happy to be indoors on this call with you. Grab a pad and pen because I'm going to dive right in with the eight marketing ideas that I promised we'd cover on this call."

Expect to generate some business from the teleclass. Focus on serving a wide audience who may not buy from you today but will appreciate your information and stick with you for the long haul. If you'd like to hear my teleclasses, you're welcome to listen to any of my recordings at Sparkandhustle.com. They may inspire ideas for your own calls.

Write the Book (Literally)

Just as I'm expanding the Spark & Hustle brand with this book, you, too, may consider marketing your expertise by writing on a subject connected to what you sell. You've seen this strategy play out time and again. The restaurant owner who publishes a cookbook. The business coach who publishes a marketing book. A nutritionist publishes a book on healthy weight loss. A consignment store owner writes money-saving fashion advice. Consider this another marketing tool. Don't expect to pay your bills from a book alone.

With more publishing options than ever before, consider whether you could reach more people, overcome sales hesitations, or generate better rapport with your market if you—literally—wrote the book on your area of expertise. Obviously you must have the time, skill and discipline to write—and it may not be tops on your agenda right now—but when and if you're ready, a book or ebook could be your calling card to opening more doors for business.

Oprah Moved On—And So Should You

Appearing on *Oprah* used to be the gold standard for celebrities, authors, self-help gurus, therapists, gadget inventors and, yes, just about every business owner. One moment in that O glow meant guaranteed success.

Many business owners believe that any celebrity or journalistic endorsement means money—and in some cases they're right. If you get that kind of exposure, leverage it for all it's worth. Put pictures of that moment on your website, use them in your sales materials and trumpet the connection in social media. I do it pretty much every time I meet a star.

But don't allow the wait for a big-name endorsement to stop you from building your own cheering section. Don't ignore the power of your current champions and fans. They can do wonders for your business.

A writer for Inc.com interviewed me in Chicago and subsequently wrote an insightful piece about Spark & Hustle. I shared and promoted links to the piece for weeks. But I kept it in perspective: I knew the success of every event I produce depends on what the attendees think of it, not the media. The women who come to my events are my cheerleaders. They share their experiences and recruit other women to come learn what I offer. That's worth more than any media coverage.

Don't get me wrong: I would have jumped at the chance to appear on *Oprah*; it definitely would have provided a huge business boost for Women For Hire and Spark & Hustle. But I owe my continued success to my hard-won and authentically grown cheering section of passionate women who sing my praises, endorse my work and fuel my credibility. I never take them for granted and I do everything I can to continuously earn their recommendations. I love them for it.

Who's in your cheering section? Do you have a list of friends and family who support your success? Current or former clients and colleagues who'll give you ringing testimonials about your service or product? Strategic partners who can champion your work to their own clients or customers? Who's talking about you, referring customers to you? Who's spreading the good word about you?

The people who give you that support are your cheering section. Keep in contact with them. Champion them and what they do. Give them referrals when you can. Give to get—it works.

PROMOTION COMMOTION

Promote yourself and your business like crazy, says Angie Dingman, owner of LoveCakes (lovecakesonline.com), a Los Angeles dessert-catering company that specializes in cupcakes. Not doing so "cost me a lot of opportunities," Angie says. "When someone offers to set out your business cards at their party, take them up on it. I didn't and I think about how many customers I might have had."

Raving Fans

Think of the people you see on the sidelines at any major game. They're cheering, talking to one another, slapping high fives and eagerly awaiting the next play. They're tweeting about their favorite players, proudly showing their allegiance. These are raving fans—and you can have them, too.

Make it about them. I love it when a sports hero makes a huge play then turns toward the fans. It's an affirmation that what happens on the field is for *them*. You should do the same. Many business owners make their success solely about themselves. They don't point to—or thank—their fans often enough. Bad move.

Acknowledge their role in your success. Thank them publicly and privately for their continued support and loyalty to you and your business. Talk to them and listen to their challenges. Respond to what they say and ask.

Keep your word. Let your cheering section know that they can count on you to do what you say you'll do. If you make a mistake, acknowledge it, apologize and correct it.

Be consistent. Let them know what they can expect of you and deliver it dependably.

Be surprising. Just when your cheering section thinks they know what to expect, change it up. Surprise them in some way. Toss them an unexpected bonus. Draw attention to their professional anniversary with you. Give them their favorite product as a birthday treat. Remember their milestones. Your fans are the fuel for your business launch and growth and have a way of multiplying quickly, which brings me to referrals.

Referrals

Referrals are, hands down, the best way to grow your business. When your fans tell their friends why they should buy from you, these referred clients approach you already knowing what you do, what you charge and why you are the best choice for them. Essentially, they enter your life and business pre-sold on buying from you. A referral will cost you far less time and money than it takes to find a new client.

But referrals—even from fans—may not just happen. You have to orchestrate a strong referral system in order to reap the unparalleled rewards it brings.

Social media expert Lena West, who runs Influence Expansion in Yonkers, New York, says, "You won't G-E-T if you don't A-S-K." You can't assume that your fans will refer you without prompting. It will happen sometimes, but not often enough to fully leverage what should and could represent a huge boost in your business income. You must ask. Unfortunately most business owners don't ask, or they ask at the wrong time, and when they do, they're asking incorrectly.

the case for serving customers with excellence

Last year when I began my exclusive "Deals" series on *Good Morning America*, I looked for interesting small businesses to feature on air. For a pet products segment, I came across dogIDs, a husband-wife company owned by Lori and Clint Howitz in Fargo, North Dakota. While the quality of their exquisite collars and leashes is exceptional, what impressed me most from the very first time we spoke was their commitment to customer service. I asked Lori and Clint to share their philosophy of doing business.

How do you continue to keep customers interested in your products? "We listen very closely to what our customers want through surveys and customer-written product reviews. Then, we plan ahead to fill product voids that our customers have identified for us. We also regularly enhance products in subtle ways by adding improvements and options to catch customers' attention."

A few unhappy online customers can kill your business with the click of their mouse if they don't like the way you treat them. How do you know if people are trashing or complimenting you? "We use Google Alerts to flag us to problems and a few other review sites, like PowerReviews, ResellerRatings, and TurnTo. We watch all of these sources religiously and when that bad egg pops up, we jump on it immediately to make sure we do everything we can to make them happy. Some people are impossible to please, but we try—and we swallow our pride regularly to do so. Online reviews are gaining more and more power and will be even more important in the future."

Let's face it, you can find a dog collar and a leash pretty much anywhere. So what is it about yours? Are they unique

or is it the way you sell them? "Our product designs are very simple but unique in functionality. We also pay attention to small details that other manufacturers don't and we promote these little extra benefits: stainless steel hardware, handcrafted in the USA and no compromise on raw material. We could buy the same materials we use overseas and increase our margins tremendously, but we see value in *not* doing so—and so do our customers. We also feel very strongly about American-made and keeping profits in the USA. I used to work at Ford so have seen firsthand how foreign products can kill our economy. I have lost count of the friends I used to work with who lost their jobs in the auto industry."

What do you do to make your business personal? "We offer information to help our customers improve their relationships with their dogs—and that information, of course, ties into our products. We let customers know that we care who they are and appreciate them coming to our site. For instance, when a customer logs in, they will see a photo of their dog—or at least their dog's breed. We are also working on much more video and written content for our 'about us' page to let people know who we are, what our values are and why we love the business we're in."

EXCEEDING CUSTOMER EXPECTATIONS

For Colleen Mook, who launched a stylish online baby clothes company, Baby Be Hip (babybehip.com), finding openings to market her products is key to growing her business, as is great customer service. One of the openings came last November when Colleen read my Facebook post about the birth of my niece, Charlotte Rae. A few days later, a lovely baby gift arrived in the mail with a note from Colleen reminding me that we had met a few weeks earlier at a conference in Philadelphia. Since unique baby products are always popular with moms, I featured Baby Be Hip on my deals segment on *Good Morning America*'s website, which resulted in hundreds of orders, most of which came from new customers.

Not a bad return on a kind—and smart—gesture, right? Colleen told me later that her main goal in sending the gift was to thank me for being gracious to her at the event. But, she said, she always looks for opportunities to send someone in the media "a product that they can actually use." In my case, I got something to give Charlotte.

Colleen says that when pitching media on Baby Be Hip, she does her research and sends personalized items to editors and producers who have babies "as opposed to just sending out random products. I've had great success doing it that way."

She also sends a photo of the product and a personal note to every customer who orders a baby gift—a nicety that ensures that the sender knows exactly what the gift they bought looks like, since it is sent directly to the recipient.

Says Colleen: "We try to exceed our customers' expectations. We can't often compete with the big guys on price, but we can with our customer service."

Ask for referrals when your clients or customers are happy with you and your product, or when they're complimenting the service they've experienced, not when you are struggling. Reaching out to them when they are most excited, instead of when you feel most needy, puts a positive spin on the request. You'll find that the referral comes much more easily on those terms.

When you're asking for referrals, don't say, "Do you know anyone who could also use these products?" The question is too general. It's hard for a fan to know where to start. Instead, ask in a way that narrows the fan's frame of reference. For instance, when talking to a client whose favorite game is Scrabble, you could ask, "Is there anyone you play Scrabble with who would love a complimentary consultation with me?" Now your fan is thinking just of the people she plays Scrabble with—and the right names will come to mind.

Referrals aren't a one-and-done task. Nurture them into an engine for new business. Take some time to consider when and how often you'll thank your referral sources. A typical thank-you is an email. Not bad, but you can be more creative.

I make many business matches and referrals and have gotten many thank-you gifts and notes. I appreciate a handwritten note explaining the benefit and outcome of the referral. My other personal favorites include an $8 purse-size mirror patterned with a four-leaf clover wishing me continued good luck; a handmade pair of earrings similar to those I often wear on TV; a bottle of orange Essie nail polish (similar to the shade of the Spark & Hustle logo) called "Braziliant," with a note saying the color and name reminded the sender of me. All simple and inexpensive, but highly customized for me, which is the greatest sign of a thoughtful gesture.

A strong referral system is based on relationships, not transactions. You keep romance fresh by changing it up. Do the same with your business relationships. Thank your fans for each referral, regardless of whether it turns into business. Call to say thanks.

Donate to a charity in a fan's name. Let your fans know in more than one way and on more than one occasion what their referrals mean to you.

Mastering the Media

The most common question I'm asked is, "How can I get on *Good Morning America*?"

ALWAYS BE READY

Never pass up a chance to get publicity, says Jeretta Horn Nord, of Entrepreneur Enterprises (acupofcappuccino.com), which inspires, educates and empowers entrepreneurs. Getting off a subway during a trip to New York City in June 2009, she saw a Fox News truck and reporter by the courthouse reporting on the Bernie Madoff scandal. "I introduced myself, saying I had the answer to economic recovery. I gave him my card," Jeretta says. "Thanks to Adam Shapiro, my first TV appearance was on Fox Business Channel shortly thereafter."

The good news is that you can get on TV without hiring a publicist. I've learned in my years on *Good Morning America* that producers are under constant pressure to develop timely pieces. The same applies in radio, newspapers, magazines and blogs, where reporters are always hunting for fresh stories. With every media platform producing content for their websites, the demand for content is greater than ever.

As such, your phone will ring if you position yourself as the go-to person in your industry. Whether you live in a big city or a small town, here are a few ways to get your number on the media's speed dial.

Start by determining which media is right for you. What makes the most sense for your business? Do you warrant national attention or would local be best? Should it be live TV, print coverage, an online piece or a radio interview—and why? Is your expertise targeted to morning show viewers or sci-fi enthusiasts? Is it consumer- or business-driven?

Then make a list of every specific outlet you'd like to target. Research each to defend (if only to yourself) why you have something of value to offer this program or print outlet. Study the types of stories they typically cover and guests they book. Look for similarities that relate to your business and rule out media outlets that aren't a good fit.

For example, many well-meaning publicists routinely pitch me stories on subjects that have nothing to do with what I cover on *Good Morning America*. I cover career issues, saving money, and consumer deals. This is obvious if you spend a few minutes Googling me or watching some of my *GMA* videos online.

Yet I continually get pitches about medical issues, pet emergencies and car problems. I delete them. Sending me a pitch about a topic other than what I cover tells me you didn't do your homework and are not worth my time.

I'm not alone here. Pitch any busy reporter on a subject that he or she does not cover and you'll get a frosty reception, too.

TELL ME A STORY

That's what Mandy Vavrinak advises clients through her business, Crossroads Communications (mandyvavrinak.com), a Tulsa, Oklahoma–based firm that helps businesses grow by sharing their stories, products and ideas. "When you're thinking about PR, think about stories. Why are you doing what you're doing, who benefits and why would anyone care?"

Do your homework. Once you know which media outlet is a good fit, find the right person to pitch by checking out their website or cold-calling to ask. Be sure you've watched and read what they are currently doing. Friend them on Facebook, follow them on Twitter and comment on the stories they are covering. All of this makes the cold call you're about to make a bit less daunting. (I'm also a contributing editor at *SUCCESS* magazine. If you're pitching me, mention a story in the current issue that you especially liked. This shows me that you know our content, which means I'm more likely to pay attention to your pitch.)

Look for slow news days, such as around holidays or hot summer weekends, when most of us prefer to be doing anything but work. For beat reporters, that translates to "no news." For you, that represents a good time—an opportunity—to pitch a story and make the reporters' lives easier while generating coverage for you.

Reach out and engage. Reporters are people, too. They like being told that you appreciate their work and that you have a great idea for them. I know because I spent years as an ABC and NBC News publicist, pitching stories to reporters all day. My favorite was a guy who wrote the TV column at *USA Today*. I liked him so much I married him and gave him two adorable kids.

Personalize your pitch. If you're pitching me a career-success-for-moms idea, write a short email outlining the story. Don't just send a one-size-fits-all press release. If your pitch resonates with my life or the stuff I cover, I'm not going to throw it away. The extra time and effort are worth it.

Once you know who to contact and how to get their attention, you need a great pitch.

An effective pitch reveals why a reporter would want to feature your story, why it makes the most sense to do so now and why the audience will care. Relay all of this information quickly and concisely. It isn't enough that you wrote a book, launched a new business or that you have something to sell. In fact, if a reporter or producer feels that you're focused primarily on sales and making money, they'll reject your pitch. Selling and making money may be key to *you*, but reporters want to know how your idea, service or product will serve *them* and *their* audience. If you're pitching me a product for a "Deals" segment, don't start off by telling me that you've got a ton of merchandise to unload. Instead, focus on why my viewers would flip for what you offer.

Be clear about your credentials so that if the topic interests them, they'll want to book you—not some other expert.

Next, make your pitch timely. Most media outlets want to connect their pieces to current events or hot trends. Figure out how you can link what you're suggesting to what's in the news. This is called having a "why now" peg to the story.

When a media outlet responds to your pitch, be ready with the points you want to make. Prepare to answer questions about your business history and your product or service, and if the segment is live, dress to best represent your brand.

Building your media profile demands a strategic, consistent effort. Keep track of the outlets you're targeting, who and what you've pitched and when you contacted them. A simple chart like the one on the next page will help you organize this information:

There are websites that tip you to stories that reporters and producers are working on right now. When you register with HARO (HelpAReporter.com), which is free, you receive three emails a day with dozens of queries from reporters seeking information, quotes and interviews for their pieces. It takes just a few minutes to scan each email. Respond to queries related to your niche or industry with tailored replies. Instead of saying, "I can address your topic. Call me," answer the query fully and specifically, and include your qualifications as an expert or details about your product or service. This will help you get coverage because you're making it easy on the reporter to see why your response stands out among others.

REWARDING AWARDS

A good way to promote yourself or your business is by seeking outside recognition, says Colleen J. Payne, who owns MCI Diagnostic Center (mobilecardiac.com), an outpatient diagnostic imaging center in Tulsa, Oklahoma. "As a small company, I couldn't afford to buy radio and TV time," Colleen says. "But I could brand myself and my company with awards and various accreditations."

Include a basic media kit on your website. This can be housed in the "About Us" section on a single page that features your high-resolution photo, a short biography, the topics you're expertly qualified to cover, any prior media coverage you've received and

media outlet	contact name	phone number	email
Good Morning America	Tory Johnson	212.290.2600	tory@ sparkandhustle .com

your contact information. Appearing media-ready is often enough to convince a reporter that you're worthy of coverage. If you're aiming for TV coverage, some bookers may want to see video of your media appearances. If you don't have any, create a video of yourself and have someone who's media savvy look at it to tell you if it's any good, then post it in this section.

Once you break through and are featured in a story—and you will if you're prepared and persistent—don't sit back and wait for orders to materialize. Market the coverage through social media and email. Make sure that you're easy to find on the Internet. People will Google you if they like what they saw or heard, so be sure they can find you and your site.

When they do, make sure you can satisfy demand. Whether ten or ten thousand people visit your site on the day of your big media debut, be prepared to capture their contact information, wow them with even more of your expertise and, if applicable, sell them your product or service.

On a smaller scale, you and your business may not warrant national TV attention and your town may have limited media out-

date contacted	pitch	notes
3/7/2012	organizing products for new moms	Not interested at this time; check back for Mother's Day.
5/4/2012	tips from mom inventors	Introduced me to a blogger for ABCNews.com for an online piece

lets. If so, think creatively about ways to generate coverage through a popular church bulletin, a leading local blog, a college radio station or a weekly *Penny Saver*. There may be organizations, such as a community bank or school, that distribute newsletters about happenings around town. All these things are opportunities to make a splash among the locals while attracting attention for your business.

If your pitches are rejected, ask for candid feedback. Is it the idea? Is it the timing? Is there anything you could do to make the idea more appealing? Sometimes you'll get a response, other times you won't, but it can't hurt to ask. Offer to work on the story and set a time when you'll check back with an update. You'll often face many rejections before you get a yes.

Securing media for your business comes down to having a media-worthy story that's timely and appeals to the right audience, making connections with the appropriate reporters or producers and being consistent with your pitches over time. This isn't a one-and-done effort; it requires patience and persistence to see your name in lights.

Networking Without Wasting Time

Even the most committed networker reaches a point when she wonders if it's worth it. Many business owners feel over-networked and underpaid, questioning whether putting themselves out there again and again will ever result in new business. Just getting your name or business out there doesn't bring in customers. But networking done right can reap benefits.

When people attend a Business Network International event, they are there to increase their sales. They enter the ballroom with

MAKE FRIENDS

Alyson Hoag of Authentic Beauty (myimagejourney.com), an Atlanta beauty and makeup company, says that if you have something valuable to say, share it. "If you have something that is going to make a difference, commit to getting your message heard instead of waiting to be discovered," she says. "Go to the trade shows to make industry contacts. Tell your existing clients and customers about it because they will talk. Make friends with people in the media and be available whenever they call. Put it on your Facebook page and watch it spread among friends."

BE YOURSELF

Be yourself to network effectively, says Jessica Rivelli, owner of Working Women of Tampa Bay (workingwomenoftampabay.com), which connects professionals through networking events. "If you come from a place of authenticity, you'll develop stronger business relationships," she says. "It's not about how many people you meet, but the quality of the conversations."

a fistful of business cards, focused on finding customers. Problem is, everyone else in the room is trying to do the exact same thing. Everyone is there to sell, not buy. No wonder it's frustrating.

I used to attend industry functions because I knew it was the thing I needed to do to get ahead. After scores of functions with no new contacts, I wondered if I needed to keep going. Successful professionals swore by them. So what was I doing wrong? I replayed the last few events in my mind and a light dawned. Although I meant business when I went to events, I acted like a wallflower at a grade school dance. I would bring a friend with me, and we'd stand off in a corner and watch the action, talking *about* everyone instead of talking *to* them. I was losing out on opportunities by clinging to my security blanket.

So I began to go alone. I set a goal for myself: I couldn't leave until I had introduced myself to at least three people. I admit that at the first several events I subsequently attended, all three people I approached were waiters. These were the easiest people for me to chat with, so I clung to them.

KNOW YOUR AUDIENCE

At a women's conference, I met a golf instructor whose business was on the rocks. When I asked what she was doing to get customers, she said she connected with new people all the time by attending speed-networking events. To figure out why this wasn't working, I asked her to recite her pitch to me, and I quickly discovered the problem. Everything she said focused on her business, not on the needs of her audience. Big mistake.

Her pitch: "Hi, my name is Jan Jones and I'm a golf instructor. I've been giving golf lessons for more than twenty years and I was trained by the top pros on the best courses in the world. I offer hourly lessons, half-day programs, and a full eighteen-hole special package. I would love to help you develop an interest in this wonderful sport. Thanks!"

Not bad. But consider who she's pitching: businesswomen looking to boost their businesses, not women looking to pick up a new sport.

With that in mind, here's what I advised her to say instead: "Hi, my name is Jan Jones. Did you know that millions of dollars in business deals happen on the golf course? If you're not out on the green, you're missing your share of that money. As a seasoned golf instructor, my specialty is getting women quickly up to par. Let's talk about how golf can grow your bottom line."

Big difference. Both are about sixty words, but one is all about her; the other is about them. She now tweaks her pitch to suit any demographic—from single women (citing the number of single men who list golf as an interest on dating sites) to women who want to lose weight (touting how many calories you burn on the driving range).

Then I pledged to myself that I had to find three other people who'd registered to attend as I did. Sometimes nothing comes of it. We exchange a mediocre handshake and an odd grin. But more times than not, I get a new nugget, resource, idea or contact that I never would have gotten had I not put myself out there. Try it. It works.

To further increase the benefit of your networking:

LOOK AT PROFITABILITY. Unless you love attending mixers, stop attending the events that don't attract your target audience.

KNOW THAT NETWORKING EVENTS ARE NOT SELL-A-THONS. They're expand-a-thons designed to make new connections.

REQUEST MORE BUSINESS CARDS THAN YOU GIVE OUT. It's fine to pass out your card, but when you request someone else's card, you're in control of the follow-up. Once home, separate the cards you've collected into categories. Give priority to contacts you can convert to clients. Some will be connections among women whose businesses relate to yours. Develop those relationships further over email and phone to see how to partner with one another. Others will be lower priority connections where you'll send a short "Great to meet with you" email and connect via social media.

Regardless of which group these cards fall into, recognize them as seeds that must be watered. Organize networking connections in a simple filing system and touch base every few months. You can send an email with a link to a relevant and interesting article about the other person's industry, congratulate that person on a recent success, or simply ask how things are going. Include a short update about your progress, too.

Talk is a cheap way to generate business, as long as your words are the right ones for the target audience.

Don't Do It Alone

It's tempting to think that no one can do things as well as we can or that it's easier to do it all ourselves. It's equally tempting to think that partnering with others is worrisome since you're not clear on what you'd offer or why anyone would send business your way when they're in need of clients, too.

Sure, you have to be comfortable relying on yourself, but if you're trying to create success in isolation, your road will be longer and lonelier than it has to be. In my business, aligning with smart colleagues and partners has been invaluable. I could not have built Women For Hire and Spark & Hustle without their support. That's why I always recommend recruiting key people to be part of your business success.

GET HELP

Nell Merlino, founder of Make Mine a Million (countmein.org), a nonprofit that helps women grow their businesses into million-dollar enterprises, is a big believer that women must reach out to others for help in growing their businesses. "You can have it all—as long as you don't do it all. We think our paw prints need to be on everything, and that can be a fatal flaw. Instead, work to have a lot of other paws working for you," Nell says. "Entrepreneurs need help. They need other people's ideas, energy and different experiences to grow their enterprise. It's a mistake to think you can do it all alone. Not only is it impossible, it's no fun."

CHAMPIONS AND BBFS

Champions are the people who encourage and inspire you and wholeheartedly support you. They may never buy from you, but they will always look for ways to promote you and remind you of your potential. These are the people who'll provide mentorship and support with no strings attached.

ABC News anchor Diane Sawyer is one of my champions, always giving me the best segment ideas and pushing me to get involved in meaningful projects that make a difference.

Atlanta event marketing executive Robyn Spizman never misses a chance to promote my events, whether I seek her help or not, and she never expects anything in return. She introduced me to book publishing and shared her literary agent with me. She routinely secures media coverage for my Atlanta events using her personal connections.

New York public relations and business development guru Heidi Krupp is constantly sharing fresh ideas to build my brand and boost my bottom line. She regularly makes introductions to people she believes would be well-served by working with me.

My daughter, Emma, talks about her BFFs all the time. You know, those best friends forever. At Spark & Hustle, I put my own twist on that: I encourage everyone to make BBFs: Business Best Friends. These are the women you'll come to lean on for advice, support and referrals to grow your business. They'll always tell it to you straight.

When thinking about BBFs, don't just surround yourself with people like you; diversify and think beyond your inner circle.

This was evident with fourteen-year-old Tori Molnar, who attended Spark & Hustle to learn the ropes as she launched Utoria, a direct sales company for young girls. She met hundreds of women, the youngest of whom was twice her age, and soaked up their advice. A few months later, she returned to our conference series—this time as a speaker. The audience expected to hear a sweet tale of a little girl's dream. Instead, they were blown away by Tori's drive and savvy as she talked about her struggle with cerebral palsy and how she chose to give up the social scene in high school in favor of cyberschool home studies so she could devote days to building her business. It was a moment of reverse

watch the caffeine

Everyone wants to "pick your brain" when you appear successful or you have a skill or expertise people want. You want to be polite, so you accept every lunch date and coffee meeting. I have a firm rule against that. Lunch dates are reserved for people who can advance my business. Sounds selfish, I know, but that's ok and here's why: meetings that help other people take hours out of your day once you factor in round trip travel and meeting time. Instead, if someone needs my help, I can save both of us a lot of time by getting on the phone for a few minutes instead of meeting face-to-face. When in-person is important, I offer time for coffee next door to my office instead of a long lunch. On the flip side, when I'm courting someone, I don't ask to have lunch unless I know I can impact their business. Otherwise, if I'm merely looking for help, I respect their time by asking for a short call or a brief coffee on that person's turf. For you, instead of accepting invitations or asking others to meet, ask yourself if you could accomplish the same result via phone or email in much less time. Have lunch only when face-to-face is the best way to serve both of you.

mentoring—a younger person inspiring and educating an older crowd. Everyone learned something about determination and perseverance in those five minutes.

I get regular emails from people who have developed their own circle of champions by attending Spark & Hustle conferences—like-minded women in unrelated businesses who root for one another's success. They share ideas, hold one another accountable and serve as cheering sections, creating buzz for one another's business. These are most definitely BBFs—Business Best Friends.

Where can you find these champions? They're at networking events, softball games and high school reunions. They may be past clients, personal friends, current colleagues, social media connections or even well-meaning family members.

Cultivate them in your business action plan. Stay connected with them, update them on what you're doing professionally and keep tabs on what they're up to. A monthly phone call or regular social media interaction can cover these bases.

Champions also need to be championed. Look for ways to encourage and support the people who champion you. While every detail is not tit-for-tat, overall it's a two-way street.

SUPPORT PARTNERS

Where do you go for help when your budget doesn't allow you to hire a full-time employee? Support partners. These are independent contractors or freelancers who can take a load of work off your to-do list. They'll free you up for more important, profit-producing tasks. They'll also fill the gap when your expertise is lacking.

Support partners may include attorneys, accountants, designers, virtual assistants, copywriters, photographers, tech gurus, social media strategists and more, depending on your business type.

To determine which tasks you should farm out, answer these questions:

Aside from sales, which should remain your responsibility as you launch and grow the business, what tasks do you dread? I'm terrible with numbers, but I recognize their importance, so bookkeeping was one of the first tasks I contracted out. As our books grew more complicated, I added a CPA in addition to a daily bookkeeper.

What business tasks do you lack the expertise to do efficiently? If you're not good at it, you'll spend too much time trying to get it done—and may not even be successful. This might include building a website—it's a necessity, but if you're challenged by it, find someone who can do it with ease.

Which tasks cause you the most headaches?

_____

Which tasks take the most time away from your core business?

_____

Which tasks do you dream of having someone else handle because you know someone else will do a better job than you can?

_____

The answers you come up with will point toward the tasks you may consider outsourcing. Remind yourself that asking for this help is cost-effective because it frees you to do what you do best.

Obviously you'll need money to farm out such tasks, but the return on those investments is likely to be strong if you select the right people at the right price. In certain situations, it's important to pay for the best—such as accounting and legal advice. Don't skimp on those, because it's likely to cost you more in the long run. In the early days of Women For Hire, I hired Dora Dvir, an accounting major at the top of her class at New York University, to help with basic bookkeeping for my fledgling company. As our needs grew, so did her capabilities and credentials. She's now a CPA and is an invaluable asset to the company and me.

For other things, you may be able to get away with less expensive—and therefore less experienced—labor. A high school student may be able to help you set up a Facebook page and Twitter account—and won't cost as much as an experienced professional.

PROFIT PARTNERS

A profit partnership is a relationship between two entrepreneurs with the primary goal of growing both businesses. You may have heard it referred to as a strategic alliance, joint venture, partnership or collaboration.

For several years, I have delivered keynote speeches at the prestigious Conferences for Women in Massachusetts, Pennsylvania and Texas. These are one-day events, each drawing more than five thousand professional women. I love the energy, and even though I am not paid to speak, I reap plenty of financial benefits: I have been hired to speak at future engagements by some of the sponsors, and many attendees become private consulting clients.

After a few of these events, program director Laurie Dalton White and I traded best practices and war stories. Laurie asked what *more* we could do together. So last year, as I began to grow Spark & Hustle, we expanded her events to two days, with the first being a small business boot camp co-branded between the Conferences for Women and Spark & Hustle. This allowed Laurie's attendees to benefit from an expanded offering and it put my new brand in front of a large, well-established audience. A win for all as we had a dual goal: inspire attendees and make money together. This wasn't a partnership for promotion; we were partners in profit, too.

Such arrangements are definitely worth pursuing when both parties can bring something of value to the table. You can continue to work alone, but new avenues of success may be possible only if you have a strong strategic partner.

Business partnerships, no matter how informal, require care and deliberation. Partner with people who share your integrity. If you question someone's motives, even slightly, don't get in bed with them. Beware of partnering with anyone who seems desperate or needy. You don't have time to handle that baggage, and such a partnership may reflect poorly on you. The last thing you want to hear is a potential client asking, "What's with your partner?" That can be the kiss of death for a deal—and your business.

The key to finding ideal profit partners is to look for people who are already serving your target market but not competing directly with you. For example, a nutritionist or acupuncturist can partner with a holistic juice bar; a career coach, with an image consultant; and a web designer, with a graphic designer, a photographer, and a social media strategist.

Another way to find potential profit partners is to consider where your clients go before they come to you or after they leave you. If you provide career training for young professionals, you can make mutually beneficial alliances with college career counselors and image consultants.

Consider offering joint promotions. For example, a new bakeshop can provide the popular shoe store down the street with coupons—one free coffee for every pair of shoes purchased. That's a no-risk gift for the shoe store and a way for the bakery to attract new customers.

Many times women say, "I am just starting out, why would anyone want to collaborate with me?" That's a question you must be able to confidently answer up front. When I launched Women For Hire, I was naturally concerned with facing an uphill battle to get Fortune 500 companies to spend money on my unknown brand. To establish immediate credibility, I partnered with *Mademoiselle*, a top magazine that catered to my demographic: women in their twenties. That allowed me to tout *Mademoiselle* as a partner in all of my pitches.

How'd I get *Mademoiselle* to say yes? When I pitched the marketing manager, I said I'd feature large *Mademoiselle* posters at my event, distribute copies of the magazine and allow their advertisers to give samples to my audience. I knew that every magazine offers advertisers added bonuses and this could be an easy one for *Mademoiselle* at no cost or hassle. In exchange, I also wanted a short blurb in the northeast edition of their magazine, promoting my first New York event. They said yes—and I scored a huge win. In addition to the ability to boast a well-known magazine as a sponsor and the in-book mention of my expo, I got mascara, lipstick, panty hose, snack bars and more to distribute in gift bags to my attendees. Who doesn't love free loot?

Another example: Women For Hire launched just one month after the debut of *The View*. Star Jones was among the original women on the daytime show. She had a new book coming out, and I offered to buy one hundred copies from the publisher if Star would attend my event for an hour-long book signing. I knew most authors couldn't sell a hundred books at a traditional bookstore signing, so this was an opportunity worth any author's time. I gave the books away through a raffle, which was an inexpensive element of fun at the expo. Buying one hundred books at wholesale for well under $1,000 was an enormous savings for me when compared to a celebrity's typical appearance fee. It was another major win for my event that helped establish credibility right out of the gate. (Incidentally, this is something I continued to do for the first three years of the company, with prominent authors who appealed to my Women For Hire audience.)

Before you pick up the phone or send off an email, identify at least three things that the other party could gain by working with you. You're probably clear about how *you* can benefit, but are you equally focused on how this will serve *them*? For example, can you help solve a headache? Can you fulfill a need? Can you offer exposure to a new audience? What specifically is the advantage of aligning with *you*? The answers may not come to you overnight, so sit on it for a few days or weeks, until you're confident about what you can offer. Only then should you reach out.

When you do reach out, avoid sounding needy. "I'm just starting out and could really use your support" doesn't instill trust or confidence, which is essential if you're asking someone to put her brand or reputation in your hands. Here's how I pitched *Mademoiselle*: "I'm a longtime subscriber of *Mademoiselle* and I have a mutually beneficial promotional partnership to propose. Specifically,

I'd like to feature your magazine at my high-profile women's career expo, and in exchange I'm looking for brief in-book exposure to make your readers aware of this exceptional free event to help advance their careers."

Never would I have said, "This is a new, yet unproven event, but I think it'll all work out." Including even a hint of negativity would have caused anyone reading my pitch to dismiss it. Don't put yourself down or be self-deprecating, and never give anyone reason to doubt your ability to deliver.

If you want to partner with a large company, determine the best person to approach. Instead of assuming it's the most senior person, such as the CEO, think about who's likely to have the greatest day-to-day involvement in the type of partnership you want. LinkedIn company pages and companies' own websites can help with contact information.

Once you have a good feel for whom to contact, identify the best method for connecting. Is this person active on LinkedIn or Twitter? Is his or her email address or phone number readily available through a simple Google search? Do you have a mutual connection who can make an introduction?

Reach out with a brief explanation of the nature of your proposal and a simple request for ten minutes of time by phone. Don't overhype your pitch with phrases like "If you give me just a few minutes of your time, I'll show you the absolute best partnership proposal you've ever seen." I'm usually cool to such language since it's invariably an empty offer. I prefer when someone is direct. For example, "I have a strong cross-promotional idea that would connect your brand with five hundred women in finance. This is a no-cost opportunity based on a shared audience, so I'm hoping you'd be willing to give me a few minutes of your time to discuss what I can do for you." If you don't hear back within a week, vary your methods of communication. Try social media. Call instead of emailing. When calling, be ready to go with your pitch if you get the person on the phone.

Discuss the parameters of your partnership at the beginning of the relationship. No detail is too small. Is it an ongoing relationship or project-based? What is the profit split, if any, and what is expected of each person? Do both parties feel the partnership is equal? If not, you may run into issues of poor follow-through, lack of support and even blatant sabotage.

As with all relationships, keep the lines of communication open. Leave room for renegotiation. An agreement for a profit split on one project doesn't mean you can assume it on all future collaborations.

Finally, distinguish if you're partnering for promotion or partnering for financial profit. I do both, depending on the people and organizations I'm working with.

Don't get lulled by extensive barters and promotional fluff. Question how any particular promotional relationship will lead to sales, either directly or indirectly. Focus on making money for your business. You have only so much time in each day and you're on a mission; spend the bulk of your efforts building a profitable business, not simply getting your name out there.

act now

- Do your own marketing. Sell yourself first, your company second and your product third.

- Use your marketing to grab the attention of your target market and get into a conversation with them.

- Know the buying habits of your niche and spread your bets by using a variety of methods to reach your target market.

- Design your website to clearly and concisely state what you do and for whom you do it. Incorporate email signups to capture the addresses of site visitors.

- Consider hosting teleclasses, writing a book, publicizing your business in the media, attending networking events and reaching out to support partners, profit partners and project collaborators.

CHAPTER EIGHT

go social

Understatement of our times: one of the best ways to market your business is through social media, a powerful and effective platform that is essential to entrepreneurs. I marvel at all the time and money that social media saves me today, compared to when I launched Women For Hire in the late 1990s. If I'd had Facebook, LinkedIn, Twitter and other online outlets then, I could have connected with far more people faster than I did solely by cold-calling HR professionals and posting paper flyers on college campuses. (Actually, Peter did the latter for me.)

Social media is not a fad: if you're not actively engaged already,

IT FUNDS MY BUSINESS

Katie O'Neill of KT Steppers (ktsteppers.com), which sells custom, personalized stepstools for kids, says she owes her success to the power of social media. "My visibility on Twitter and Facebook pretty much funds my business," Katie says. "I wouldn't have grown as quickly if it weren't for them."

there's no excuse for not starting today. Some platforms may disappear, but social media is here to stay. Ignore it at your peril.

Social media is the easiest way to reach more people in less time than ever before. It gives you the stage, exposure and reach you need—paralleling or surpassing results that traditional media opportunities afford you.

The number of people who actively use social media dwarfs the number of viewers and readers of most traditional media, which is why TV and newspapers are desperate to engage us any way they can on the Web. They see the appeal and know it's part of their immediate and long-term future.

The best part about marketing through social media—my favorites are Facebook, Twitter, LinkedIn, Pinterest, Instagram and YouTube—is that all people have an equal voice to connect with anyone, build influence, lead a tribe or develop a cheering section for themselves and their business.

Social media puts all of this in your direct control. No press agent, published book or national media coverage needed.

Make It Work

Before you launch your social media strategy, decide what success looks like to you. While having plenty of fans, friends and followers is exciting, don't view that alone as a barometer of future success.

Certainly, more fans, friends and followers means more people to share your message with, which is a good thing. But numbers alone won't generate revenue unless they represent the right people, the ones with whom you can engage and to whom you can sell effectively because they care about what you offer.

Sign Up, Sign In

There are countless social media sites for you to join. As a starting point, I recommend using Facebook, Twitter and LinkedIn. It's worth creating accounts on other major sites, too, including You-Tube, Pinterest, foursquare, Tumblr and Instagram, if only to initially claim your business name.

I spend the bulk of my time on the first three. It's much better to go deep on a few key platforms than to barely skim the surface on too many. Facebook is effective because it's a worldwide get-together, providing a convenient and relatively informal venue for you and the rest of your world to interact, support and cheer one another, offer advice, share resources, and, of course, do business. If you sell a product directly to consumers, Facebook is a great place to raise your flag. You can use text, photos and video all in one place .

On Twitter, you can post quick updates, provide links to pictures, share and receive advice and more, but your reach is fleeting because of the speed in which the content feed moves. It's the digital cocktail party, where quick bits of your expertise can be exchanged with anyone who values it and you can meet others in your field. Maximize the available real estate by customizing your Twitter background to reflect your brand.

LinkedIn is the most professional network of the three. While Twitter and Facebook both offer a fun vibe, LinkedIn is more formal and, as such, more serious. If you sell products or services to professionals or businesses, LinkedIn is for you. In addition to creating your personal profile, you should create a group for your business or a company page. Search and join groups that relate to your field. Get active with LinkedIn Answers, where you can demonstrate your expertise by answering questions that are relevant to all that you know.

We all love visuals. They're a powerful way to easily connect with an audience. I love image-sharing network Pinterest (pinterest.com), which is a virtual bulletin board where you can *pin* (or tag) images that you like while surfing the web or those that you upload on your own. The offline analogy is much like flipping through a magazine, ripping out pages when you spot images you love, and tacking them to a bulletin board. Pinterest enables you to do that on the Web—creating inspiration boards categorized by topics of your choice. One of mine is called "Color of 2012." Anytime I'm online, whether I'm shopping or researching, I pin anything I find that mirrors the bright orange of the Spark & Hustle logo. I also have a board called "Spark & Hustlers of 2012," where I pin images from the websites of my event attendees. These are unique ways for me to interact with my followers while spreading the word about what we do. Search the vast network for boards that relate to your business and style to find inspiration on getting started. Whole Foods and *Real Simple* magazine, for example, are frequently cited for their expertise in using Pinterest to build community around their brands. Whole Foods does this by sharing photos of delicious recipes and you can be sure the ingredients are found in their stores. *Real Simple* inspires with a wide variety of design projects that create greater connectivity to its readers.

Another photo-sharing site to give and get inspiration is Instagram (instagram.com), which is to photos what Twitter is to 140 characters of text. The service allows you to instantly upload from your phone photos that can then be followed by anyone. If you create or sell products, this is a friendly way to share images of all that you do and offer. If you have a service business, post pictures that best represent you and your brand.

There are a variety of programs that will automate your online presence, allowing you to pre-schedule posts, but I don't use or recommend them. There is no value in pretending to be engaged online. In order to get more customers through social media, you must show up yourself to speak, respond, ask questions, make connections and share what you know.

To do this, there are two key components: what will you say and to whom will you say it? Magic happens only when you merge the two successfully.

Content

Determine your strategic purpose for being online. Mine is two-fold: driving attendance at my Women For Hire career expos and registrations for my Spark & Hustle conferences. But if all I did was say, "attend this," "register for this," or "buy this," my fans, friends and followers would flee fast.

So instead I give to get, which I do happily and with transparency—another social media must. This means I don't hide the fact that I want people to attend my events and support my products and services. I am up-front and open about it. But I also give in a wide variety of ways, including:

➤ Answering job-seeker questions

➤ Helping small business owners with a variety of challenges

➤ Sharing articles and links that both groups find interesting

- Celebrating and promoting my clients
- Soliciting feedback on story ideas for my segments on *Good Morning America* and my columns in *SUCCESS*
- Asking for insights on topics relevant to my audience
- Offering tidbits on what's happening in my life personally as it relates to the people I serve

As a side note, the biggest response I ever got to a post was when Peter broke his foot after falling from a ladder one summer. (Actually, he claims the ladder slid out from under him. Right.) I told the story of what happened—and how he may have been in agony, but as the nursemaid I didn't have it so easy, either. I asked my social media connections, "Who has it worse, the patient or the caregiver?" I needed an injection on humor on this hot summer day.

I never anticipated the feedback I got. Not only did we drive results businesswise that week because several people, comfortable using that icebreaker, began chatting with me, but I also received dozens of suggestions on every potion, lotion and cure known to mankind to help Peter's foot. Notes, gifts, advice and, yes, sales. People like to buy from people they can relate to personally.

(Incidentally, if business is ever really slow, perhaps it'll be time for Peter to break his *other* foot to, you know, take one for the team.)

In all seriousness, I typically use an 80/20 ratio when developing content to share: 80 percent of my activity is all about serving other people, while just 20 percent is directly selling and promoting my business. I have found that my audience is very receptive and grows daily as a result of that split. They appreciate that I give a lot of my time and talent to help them, and they reward me by becoming loyal followers, cheerleaders and clients.

social media do's and don'ts

DO

Be genuine and honest

Share your expertise

Invite and answer questions on topics where you can help

Find common interests on hot topics such as TV shows and movies

Promote people and businesses that you support

Provide personal experiences that relate to your audience

Celebrate the accomplishments of your fans, followers and clients

DON'T

Sell excessively

Over-share personal problems or complain

Delve into hot-button political issues

Post offensive content

Argue publicly with your followers

Trash your competitors

Skip weekends since Saturday afternoon is an especially popular time for sharing on some social sites

Daily interaction is essential if you expect to find success in this space. The more you interact, the more traction you'll get from your content. Social media search engines reward this type of engagement by exposing your content to more people. When you disappear for weeks, expect your followers to do the same.

I offer a healthy balance of personal and professional content. My personal content typically relates to my family, which is relevant since a significant portion of my followers are working moms who appreciate insights on managing work and everything else in life. I think often about Barbara Bradley Baekgaard's father's advice: you have to sell yourself before you can sell your product, service or business. Showing that side of me has strengthened my online relationships, which in turn fuels my professional success.

If you're worried about being overwhelmed by the necessary commitment to your social media pages, keep your interaction consistent by creating a content grid, which is a calendar of planned postings with ideas of the content you'll share that day. By planning ahead, you can eliminate some of the natural pressure that comes from having to generate frequent, meaningful content on the spot. You can certainly be spontaneous and respond to what's going on each day, while still sharing your scheduled content on time. Don't be afraid to schedule in a free day. Take Sunday off or use it as a day to plan the week ahead, if you'd rather plan out one week at a time instead of the month ahead.

SAMPLE CONTENT GRID

A content grid is essentially a weekly or monthly calendar. Instead of appointments, the space is filled with the educational, interesting or enriching content that you'll post daily on Facebook, Twitter, LinkedIn or the sites of your choice. Don't be so scripted that you lose all spontaneity, but do plan ahead so you're not paralyzed by what to post on any given day. Here are a few ideas to get you started.

- Themed days (Make it Happen Monday)
- Contests and polls
- Quotes and resources (Friday Favorite)
- Get fifty specific ideas for content at Sparkandhustle.com/book

Connections

Whom should you connect with? Just as in your personal life, where you don't befriend everyone on the street, you want to focus on the right connections in business. The best place to start is with people you already know:

- Friends and family
- High school and college alumni connections
- Coworkers, former colleagues, clients, customers, vendors and suppliers

that's all it takes

Social media engagement need not take up all of your time. You should spend twenty minutes each weekday morning on your social business networking and marketing, says social media guru Jennifer Abernethy. "Then move on."

Content Grid May

monday	tuesday	wednesday
	1	2
7	8	9
14	15	16
21	22	23
28	29	30

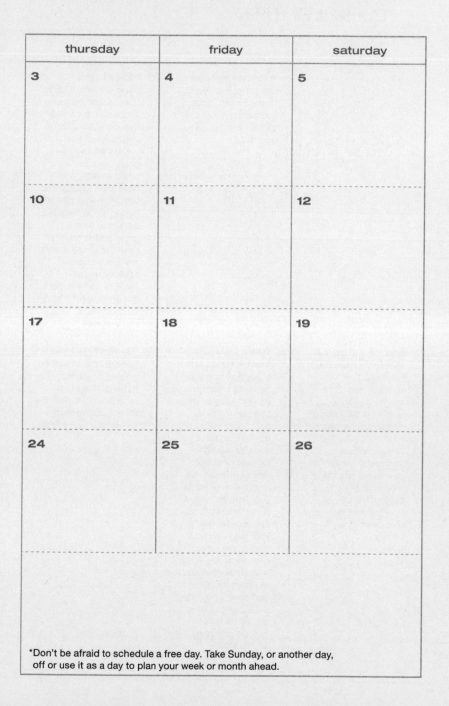

thursday	friday	saturday
3	4	5
10	11	12
17	18	19
24	25	26

*Don't be afraid to schedule a free day. Take Sunday, or another day, off or use it as a day to plan your week or month ahead.

Content Grid May

monday	tuesday	wednesday
	1 REVIEW Offer your candid opinion on a current event, book, product or movie that's closely connected to your field.	**2 REVEAL** Get personal. When I talk about small business success, I'm candid that my interest in entrepreneurship started when I was coldly and unexpectedly fired from a job I loved. The scar from that pink slip forced me to want one person or one organization never to have the ability to strip me of my financial security or self-esteem, so I ventured out on my own. Share your personal experiences, too.
7 GIVE Give a special offer to your fans and followers. For example, this document you're reading is something I offered to give away—no strings attached. You can create something similar for your target market or even give a special discount or bonus offer for a limited- time on a product or service.	**8 TIPS** It is especially relevant for experts to share their expertise regularly by posting a tip of the day or week. Use tips that are actionable and avoid being generic—e.g., if you're talking to job-seekers, "Join and participate in a discussion group in your field on LinkedIn" is better than "Use social networks for your job search." It also works for product manufacturers— e.g., if you make brownies, share cooking tips. Someone who sells an organizer can offer tips on tackling various rooms in simple steps.	**9 RE-POST** Re-tweet or re-post tips, thoughts, articles or other material that others have posted online. Be sure to acknowledge where you saw it first.

thursday	friday	saturday
3 REPORT Conferences and events offer rich material to share through social media. You can post quotes, tips, take-aways and photos from the speakers and sessions. Allow others to participate vicariously through you.	**4 PROMOTE** Promote something you're working on—a book, a product, a project, an article, an event, you name it—and let people know where to learn more. This is also true for your blog posts and stuff on your website. Promote it through social media to bring people directly to your site.	**5 SHARE** When you read an article in the morning paper, find a link to the piece online and share it with your networks. The same is true for any great content or resource you find online. When I read magazines, I dog-ear pages to share tidbits online.
10 INSPIRE Let everyone know how you've overcome a challenge and share how they can do it, too.	**11 ASK** Pose a question that relates to your field and is likely to generate strong reaction. This can be very wide-ranging.— e.g., I posted on my Facebook wall: "A woman told me she's changing her hair color to 'look smarter.' Do you think hair color impacts our perception of intelligence?" (That got *a lot* of reaction.) On Twitter I ask viewers to submit ideas for my TV segments.	**12 EXPLOIT** Have a pet peeve? Exploit it. One of mine is selling from the stage at business conferences, which leads to a feeling of letdown once home, realizing that what you paid for wasn't delivered, wasn't made actionable or didn't help your bottom line. It's a reminder to me when promoting my events that I must explain why my programs are different.

Content Grid May

monday	tuesday	wednesday
14 SHOWCASE If you have a great client success, feature it. When someone I work with gets a new job or has a big win in her business, I showcase those successes online. It also serves as a testimonial for your work and your expertise.	**15 SOLICIT** Ask for feedback on a trend in your line of work or feedback on an element of something you're working on. Everyone loves to offer an opinion.	**16 MORNING** Consider posting a morning greeting each day that is relevant, fun, interesting or challenging. It may be connected to current events—Did you watch X show last night? Are you going to the polls to vote today? Do you know what happened this day in history?—instead of directly related to your work.
21 RECOMMEND Let your fans, followers, friends and connections know why you recommend a particular product or service. Include a link to it.	**22 LAUGH** A clean (non-offensive) joke is always welcome.	**23 CONTEST** Ask everyone to submit something. A staffing firm can ask fans to submit the most challenging interview question they've ever faced. An accessories company can ask women to submit photos of the inside of their bag. Combine and share the content in a clever way.

thursday	friday	saturday
17 PERSONALIZE While most of your content will be professional, give some personal details to share another side of you. I got a huge reaction when I shared my husband's foot injury that left him in pain—and me exhausted from being ordered around! I talk about my kids. I stressed over turning forty. It allows my audience to know me better—and hopefully feel a stronger connection with me.	**18 THEME** Use daily, weekly or monthly themes to inspire regular content. An organic baker might implement a thirty-day "Make Your Friends Green with Envy" campaign with tips on keeping your pantry stocked with clean foods. Or maybe it's Motivational Mondays. Or Wellness Wednesday, which can encompass a range of content. A theme allows you to build out the content in advance to fit the days.	**19 CONTROVERSY** Rather than polarizing your connections with a personal rant, consider posting a question about a controversial hot topic. I did this on the Oklahoma governor's race between two female fifty-something candidates—one married with six kids, the other single, no kids. The married mom said she was more qualified because of her marital and parenting status, so I asked my followers to chime in.
24 CHALLENGE Issue a challenge to your audience. I've challenged my followers to make cold calls each day to five people who they've held back on reaching out to—and I've encouraged them to share the feedback with me on how it goes.	**25 PHOTOS** Poke around other people's pages and profiles and study the ones that use many photos. Force yourself to capture moments with your cell phone or digital camera at work that others will enjoy. Once you get in the habit, it becomes easier to find stuff to share.	**26 PROVE** Include a brief "case study" showing where a client started, what you did, how you did it, and the results that were experienced. You can also do the same as an employee or job-seeker based on the work you do.

Content Grid May

monday	tuesday	wednesday
28 VIDEO Even more powerful than photos, create original videos to share. The popularity of YouTube should be enough to convince you that video is an extraordinary way to get your message across. Many of the elements on this chart can be recorded by you on video and shared, especially if you have a built-in recorder on your computer or phone.	**29 HIGHLIGHT** Highlight a blog that you follow and tell your audience why you believe they'd like it, too.	**30 GIFT** Send a book or promotional item to the first five or ten people who respond to a specific call to action.

The next step is friending and following people you want to get to know. Again, be strategic when choosing these new connections. Some ideas:

➤ Ten companies serving your market, but not competing directly with you, and people who work there

➤ Luminaries and leaders in your field, including the people you've long admired and always wanted to meet

➤ Potential clients or customers you want to get to know based on their use of keywords connected to your field

Use the simple search functions on each site to find, follow and friend. That is not a difficult process once you start doing it.

(Search.Twitter.com is invaluable for finding people by topic interest in Twitter.) Of course I hope you'll start by connecting with me at Facebook.com/Tory and Twitter.com/ToryJohnson. I also have a Tory Johnson group on LinkedIn and virtual vision boards at Pinterest.com/ToryJohnson.

As you're building your lists, don't sacrifice quality of engagement for quantity of connections. It's useless to have thousands of random contacts who have no real connection to you or interest in the product or service you offer.

If you're not already familiar with these sites or you're having trouble getting started, use their Help features. You can Google written and video tutorials for every social media platform. Ask a young person to set you up and guide your progress. I'm especially fond of LinkedIn's small business resource center, which features step-by-step tutorials, along with solid advice on going deep to build your digital identity on the site.

BE ORIGINAL

Get social by using social media, says Shannon Hurst Lane, who runs Traveling Mamas (travelingmamas.com), which provides travel inspiration and advice for consumers and businesses. If writing is a challenge, "take a writing class at a local community college, then develop a blog where you post something at least once a week about what inspires you. Be original and consistent."

20 ideas for social media engagement

1. Customize a Facebook landing page and adjust settings to require users to "like" it before they can comment.
2. Integrate your email newsletter sign-up on your Facebook landing page.
3. Post photos on Facebook of new products in development and ask fans to provide feedback. Involve them in naming the product or choosing a color when applicable. For a service business, post photos of yourself at work. A graphic designer might post a photo of the vision board she created for a specific project. A dog walker can post photos of pooches.
4. Keep your personal profile separate from your business page as you grow your small business, especially if your company has a distinct brand.
5. Arrange with other business owners to cross-promote by introducing your Facebook fans and followers to their products or services, and request that they do the same for you.
6. Share with fans and followers exclusive deals that can only be found on your Facebook page.
7. Customize your Twitter background with photos and text that support your product or service.
8. Link to your website from the brief bio on your Twitter page.
9. Develop a comfortable mix of personal and professional tweets designed to allow your prospects to get to know, like and trust you.
10. Host a Twitter Chat for your followers to expand your sphere of influence. Melinda Emerson (@smallbizlady on Twitter) hosts great Twitter chats for small business. I loved being her guest during an evening chat last year.

11. Create a group on LinkedIn for your business and join groups in your industry. Create a company page to showcase your offerings and interact with followers.

12. Respond to questions on LinkedIn Answers to demonstrate your expertise.

13. Using the camera on your phone or computer, record frequent video messages that showcase your expertise and post directly to YouTube and Facebook. For a service business create videos sharing your expertise. For a product-based business showcase your products and share tips and advice.

14. Create a customized YouTube channel to house all of your videos. Look at popular YouTube channels in your field and study their pages to learn best practices. (This is helpful for all of your social media pages).

15. Claim a vanity URL that matches your business name in the same format on Facebook, Twitter, LinkedIn, Pinterest, Instagram and other growing social networks that apply to your business. Get to know which site(s) are best suited for connecting with your target market.

16. Use a professional head shot and beautiful photographs on your profile pages.

17. Commit to posting regular content, the majority of which should offer value instead of selling. Integrate content by sharing your posts across all platforms. For example, I might tweet a link to a video that I shared on Facebook. I also integrate my Pinterest updates on my Facebook Timeline.

18. Use a professional email account that matches your business domain, not AOL or Gmail.

19. Avoid posting or commenting on offensive content that can tarnish your brand or alienate your followers.

20. Be genuine in all you post since people flee from fake.

Go Online to Get Them Offline

Once you've attracted your target market and they have shown an interest in your products or services through consistent conversation, take the chatter offline. Schedule a phone call, meet face to face or carry on through private email.

HAVE YOUR OWN STANDARDS

Blogs are the rage these days, but writing one can be a challenge and you can't just spew, says Grace Boyle, author of *Small Hands, Big Ideas* (smallhandsbigideas.com), a Boulder, Colorado–based Generation Y blog. "I really thought I would write whenever I wanted, but when you build an audience and subscribers, you are held accountable."

Blogging for Business

While writing a blog isn't essential, especially if you're not a writer or don't have the patience to write often, it can be another vehicle for promoting your expertise.

Wendy Piersall, author of *Mom Blogging for Dummies*, encouraged Chicago Spark & Hustle attendees to look at blogs as very public business cards with the clout to draw new customers. She said a blog can position you and your products or service as the go-to solution for your target market.

Your blog does that with valuable, searchable content that brings your market to you, allowing people to hang around and get to know you before they consider engaging in a sales conversation. Call it digital window-shopping.

In addition to or in lieu of writing your own blog, submit

articles to well-read industry blogs. Whether your expertise is rescue dogs, vegan cooking or ecommerce, there are sites that could
use your content. Share your expertise by writing frequent posts
and responding to others on reputable blogs that serve the same
audience.

You can incorporate your blog within your website or start a
separate one using www.wordpress.com or www.tumblr.com.
Tumblr allows the Internet novice to create a branded account and
offers a very easy method for updating your blog with simple
posts in the form of photos, quotes, excerpts or short paragraphs.
It's a very visual platform where color and short bursts of information do best. WordPress offers a number of templates for a blog
that can be hosted under your own domain, but requires some
skill to make it look professional and consistent with your brand.
If you've never done this before, research tutorials, take a course
or hire someone to help.

Video Marketing

In 2011, YouTube got three billion views per day, making it the
Web's second most popular search engine behind Google. That
means you should be there. I know it's intimidating for anyone
who's camera shy, but trust me: you, too, can create video right
now with an iPhone, webcam or digital-video camera. The more
you do it, the easier it gets.

With video marketing, don't worry about slick or perfect.
Focus instead on making it real and short—ideally less than two
minutes. Even big-budget, big-name businesses use unpolished
videos to market products, often finding them more profitable
than high-gloss commercials. J.Crew and Zappos feature real

people instead of models and actors, to create videos that relate to their market. You should be doing the same thing, whether you build websites, make handbags, coach job-seekers or sell cosmetics.

Many people feel uncomfortable on camera. They don't like the way they look or they fear appearing stiff and nervous. Communications expert Ruth Sherman (ruthsherman.com) works with corporate CEOs, celebrities and small business owners to master video. Her formula: practice + experience = spontaneity. In other words, creating great videos, just like effective writing and speaking, takes time. Don't expect overnight miracles, but with commitment comes results.

Videos are great for providing quick tips, bits of advice or nuggets of information in your area of expertise. A jewelry designer can offer simple two-minute videos about creative accessorizing—using her own products. A coach can make a list of twenty frequently asked questions and answer each one individually. There's no industry or business that can't benefit from video marketing. Make a list of possible topics or video ideas that you can talk about with ease.

Once you create a video, market it to generate viewers. Create a YouTube channel for your company and follow YouTube's tutorials about naming and tagging your videos with relevant keywords. Include a link to the video on your website, Facebook page, Twitter feed and LinkedIn profile. You can add a link in your email signature. Look for opportunities to promote your videos on relevant blogs and in your enewsletters.

"No time" is no excuse for skipping out on social media. Make it part of your daily routine and you'll reap the rewards if you do it right. If you use a smartphone, download apps that make it possible to connect and engage while on the go. Don't give up before

you get going: everyone starts with one fan, one friend, one fol-
lower. Hustle to build from there. The potential payoff is huge:
ignoring this marketing vehicle is not an option.

act now

- Social media platforms are an essential way to reach more people in less time than ever before. They give you the stage, exposure and reach you need to grow a small business.

- Plan to go deep on two or three sites that have the deepest
  concentration of users in your target market.

- Before you launch your social media strategy, decide what success will look like to you and how you'll measure it.

- Be a generous social networker and don't simply ask for sales.
  Nobody likes a beggar, so plan to give to get.

- Once you've attracted your target market and they have shown
  an interest in your products or services through consistent conversation, take the chat offline by meeting in person, talking by
  phone or communicating by private email.

CHAPTER NINE

||||||||||||||||||

sold is the best
four-letter word

Take a look in the mirror. If you can't sell yourself on yourself, turn back to Chapter One to get reacquainted with your spark. You must feel in your bones that what you're selling is absolutely worth the price you're charging. Sure, your confidence will wobble at times. That's when you can turn back to your one-page business plan to remind yourself of what you're on a mission to accomplish and how you'll make it work.

When I launched Women For Hire, I had no experience with, or connections to, human resource executives, the go-to folks in corporate recruiting. I had no experience putting on events, no history of success in this field, no gauge of what would work, no benchmarks to measure my progress against.

I was flying blind.

I was terrified that only twenty-five vendors and a hundred job-seekers would show up at my first career expo, which I held in a cavernous concert hall built to hold thousands of people. I panicked that I wouldn't be able to sell enough recruiting booths to cover my costs and I'd have to cancel the whole thing, losing all of my start-up money and forcing me back into an undesirable corporate job. I lay awake many nights wondering what I had gotten myself into. At times, I found myself wondering why I hadn't come up with an easier business idea.

Could I share any of my uncertainty, fear and doubt with the prospects I was pitching or the vendors I had secured? How about the media I wanted to cover the event or the job applicants I was trying to lure to attend?

Hell no. Of course not.

Back then, I chose to face my self-doubt by repeatedly—I'm talking daily, sometimes hourly—selling myself on what I was doing, the impact it would have, and the fact that I could pull it off successfully if I stayed focused. I also kept my "why" front and center, knowing that going back to get a "real" job wasn't an option.

I was determined to not fail and even more focused on success. Fire in my belly? I had a blast furnace going. I *still* have those flames burning today, and I think it's one of the main reasons for my continued success. I do not give up. I plan my agenda each day and I go after it with a vengeance.

You should do the same thing. Customers can smell fear, just

KEEP YOUR CONFIDENCE UP

Value your expertise, says Grace Kang, who runs Pink Olive (pinkolive.com), specializing in whimsical gifts for happiness and home. "Treat a much-needed service just as you would a valuable product. If you have a service that can save someone time and money, you are doing them a disservice not sharing your expertise. You're also cheating yourself by not placing a premium on the value of it."

as dogs and children do. Uncertainty makes them question if they should buy your products or enlist your services. It can greatly diminish your profit potential.

My need to sell didn't disappear after that first successful career expo. It's always front and center. It shows up when I'm launching something new. It presents itself when the economy dips. It's here when long-term clients announce budget cuts that directly impact the work they do with me.

Here are some of the techniques I use to keep pushing on:

Surround yourself with positive feedback. Many business owners use testimonials to build their credibility in the marketplace and sell to others. For me, this includes notes and emails I receive thanking me for the work I'm doing, or for the impact my advice has made on someone's life or business. These informal testimonials are all on my bulletin board, on the wall next to my desk. Surround yourself with them to sell yourself on yourself and reinforce your confidence in what you're doing.

See your motivation. I also surround myself with cards, letters and emails from people who are struggling with layoffs, financial insecurities and hard times with their businesses. These notes remind me that what I'm doing matters. They give me the sense of urgency I need to keep going on days I'd rather hang back and coast. These notes go up on the bulletin board, too.

Don't wait for a crisis to have these personal pep talks. Get in

SPEAK CANDIDLY AND HONESTLY

Honesty sells, says Marianne Carlson of Emcie Media (emcie.com) in DeLand, Florida, which creates websites and Internet marketing campaigns. "Your reputation is your single greatest asset. One unhappy customer does more harm than ten happy ones do good."

the habit of selling yourself before every key conversation or networking event. Talk frequently to that pretty gal in the mirror.

Need to see how it's done? There are two very popular YouTube videos featuring kids giving themselves a pep talk—a girl in front of the mirror and a young boy about to ride a bike. Visit Sparkandhustle.com/book for links. In a just a few minutes, you, too, will be motivated to just do it.

Know that as you move forward, you won't have to do this every day. Your confidence muscle will build as your bottom line grows.

Focus on Your Customer

Consumers are increasingly adept at ignoring sales pitches, commercials and ads—whether it's hanging up on phone solicitations or clicking the remote during TV commercials. Yet, amazingly, many sales pitches rely on dumb scripts and a laundry list of features designed to lure you into buying—when a far more effective sales tool is focusing exclusively on the customer and the benefits to him or her. Don't simply rattle off the features of what you're selling: apply each benefit to your potential customer's perceived or spoken need.

Your Top 50 List

When I decided to host my first-ever Spark & Hustle retreat for twenty established small business owners, I didn't simply create the offer, email it to the masses and wait for the phone to ring. Before I announced the program, I created a list of fifty women I felt were ideally suited for the three-day intensive. I emailed and called each of them to share details.

I used the same strategy when I launched Women For Hire and began planning my first career expo. I made a list of fifty companies I dreamed of doing business with and that I felt would get the most value out of my event. Then I reached out to each of them.

Some people on both lists said no for any number of reasons. When they did, I'd cross them off and add new names—always ensuring that I was working from a master list of fifty targeted women or companies. I never had to wonder about whom I might reach out to on any given day. The lists kept me focused and on task.

Before I make calls or send emails, I know exactly what I'm going to say and why a specific company or person might benefit from what I'm offering.

When I started this with my career expos, executives on the other end of the phone could have easily dismissed my event and me: neither of us had any track record. But I'd like to think that many of the people I spoke with recognized and appreciated that I had done my homework. I explained exactly how Women For Hire could serve them. As a result, they took it on faith that I would deliver. And I did.

When I launched Spark & Hustle, I followed the same process—explaining to current and aspiring women entrepreneurs the topics we would cover and what we would deliver over the course of three days. Many attendees told me that they signed up because my staff and I answered all their questions and concerns promptly. A good number of them said we delivered *more* than we promised, that the conferences were even more fulfilling and nurturing than they'd expected. That felt good.

ONE-ON-ONE DIALOGUE

Respect your clients, says Jessica Constable of Jess LC in Chicago (jesslc .com), which offers graceful and affordable jewelry. "Send a personal email thanking customers for their purchase and giving them the ship date. Start a one-on-one dialogue."

Instead of simply marketing to the masses—hoping you get some nibbles and maybe a few sales—approach each product or service strategically. Continue your more broad-stroke marketing efforts, of course, like posting on Facebook, blogging, creating videos for YouTube, attending networking functions and pursuing media coverage, but reach out to each of those fifty prospects directly.

The list will evolve over time. When you get a no or when you make a sale, cross that name off your list and replace it with a new one. Ask for referrals and add them to the list. This keeps your prospect pipeline full and flowing.

JUST GO DO IT

"The best way to learn to sell is to go out and sell," says legendary business leader Jack Nadel, a giant in the promotional products industry, who funded a generous scholarship program for Spark & Hustle attendees. "There's no substitute for actually doing it. The experience of being rejected may have more value than instant success. 'Trial' and 'Error' are the two greatest sales instructors."

Perfecting Your Pitch

"If I could tell you three ways to make a million dollars this year without much effort, would you be interested?"

"I see you're making a lot of mistakes in this area. I'd be happy to have a confidential conversation with you to show you what I'm doing."

"If I could show you how to lose twenty pounds just by using this special blender, would you want to know more?"

I don't know about you, but all of these pitches make me cringe. They're set up to end in one of two ways: yes or no, sale or no sale. No room for follow-up or relationship building. With such opening lines, you're making assumptions that may not be accurate. The prospect will be insulted by the notion of making so much money with little effort, bugged by the audacity of assuming she's making mistakes and offended by the insinuation that she has to lose weight. No benefit to any of that.

Never go in completely cold, even if you're cold-calling. Research your target market and know something about them before calling or showing up at their door. Look at their website, Google them, visit their Facebook page. A landscaper would check out the yards before calling with a quote, right? All initial conversations must relate directly to their needs.

Before you call, know which key questions to ask and exactly what information the person on the other end will want to know. If you're cold-calling clients to learn more about them, be ready with two or three key questions. When you're face-to-face, the other person is more likely to spend time answering your questions. But when it's by phone, expect that person to be more wary of taking what often feels like a lengthy survey.

Avoid "now or never" tactics. Consumers often need time to consider each and every purchase, regardless of size. Even though

how to call someone cold

Establish first that you're talking to the right person. For example, "I believe you're responsible for making decisions about the company's diversity recruiting efforts, correct?" Then be clear that you're not about to launch into a twelve-minute pitch. "I'm only going to take a minute of your time to introduce you to a women's career expo that'll be in Chicago in October. Since many of the leaders in your industry participate with us, I want to be sure you have the details on the program so you can consider joining us as well." This makes it local and relevant, and lets your prospect know that his or her competitors will be there. That invites conversation. At this point, you'll either offer to continue with details, email information, answer questions or call back at a more convenient time. Pause naturally to allow the other person to get a word in if she or he has something to say.

After the first Women For Hire event, I had more meat to add to my sales pitch. I used the full list of participating employers to tout my client roster, and I paid particular attention to mentioning direct competitors when pitching a new prospect. I boasted that one thousand talented women came through our doors, and I was able to share the names of the top schools they represented, along with their backgrounds and areas of expertise. I talked at length about the organizations that proudly promoted the event to drive attendance. I shared photos of the crowded event, with women dressed in business attire and beautiful displays that big-brand recruiters had set up. All of that became part of my subsequent pitches and it's what we continue to use today.

you want the sale right now, respect and honor the need for time to make a decision.

When you face repeated rejection, avoid lapsing into a defeatist, "nobody's buying" mentality. Instead, get to know your prospects better. Invite them to speak with a satisfied customer. Offer a trial. Ask if you can follow up in a week or so. Look for alternative ways to stay in an authentic sales conversation, rather than pushing for a premature close.

Determine if there is a real need. It's not enough for you to know they have a need; they must acknowledge it, too.

Instead of hinting, ask directly for the sale. Far too many business owners have a list of what they consider hot prospects, yet they've never asked them to *buy* anything. The right time to ask for the sale is after the person has acknowledged they have a need that you can fill and your solution has been discussed. Often your prospect will suggest moving forward with you. If not, be willing to ask, "Would you be interested in trying this?" Or "Does one of the options we've discussed sound appealing?" Be direct.

LET THEM GET TO KNOW YOU

If you're a coach or consultant, the best and most generous way to ask somebody to work with you is to let them get to know you, says Lisa Claudia Briggs of Intuitive Body (intuitivebody.com), which provides simple solutions for living beautifully in your body. "This is a trust-based relationship," Lisa says. "Reach out through ezines, blogs and social media. Call prospects and talk about how you will solve their problems. Don't sell. Give them that experience."

This strategy is hardly new. Car sales associates take you on a test drive, retail shops have fitting rooms and perfume spritzers offer you a sniff before you have to pull out your wallet. All of this is taste marketing.

Think about how you can allow your target market to get an accurate taste of your product or service. The freebie shouldn't be exactly what you intend to sell them, but it should hint at the benefits of doing business with you. For example, when you walk into an ice cream shop, you can taste a teeny spoonful of any flavor, but nobody hands you a full cone with two scoops to try.

Here are some tips for putting together a successful taste-test program:

Learn from the experts. Look at how the top five bloggers, salespeople or gurus in your industry start conversations on their websites. What are they talking about? Do they have a free taste offer of their own? What is it? It may be a sample, an ebook or a complimentary call.

Answer key questions: What do your prospective clients want? Why do they want it? What are they most hoping to get from it?

You may sell nutritional supplements and organic juices, but you notice most potential clients begin conversations with you by admitting they want to lose a few pounds. This could be an opportunity to offer a complimentary tip sheet on meal planning for weight loss. That gives them a taste of your style and expertise and may lead them to buy from you because they appreciate the advice.

There's no value in providing a taste to your market if, in reality, all you're doing is selling. Peter's parents once spent a free night in a new condominium in New York City. They knew that in accepting the free night, they'd commit to hearing a sales pitch. But they were insulted the following morning when a salesman delivered an intense, ham-fisted hard sell. You want your taste to be something that people are thrilled to recommend to others:

generous, fun, impactful, creative or results-oriented, so that people are inclined to share the experience. This may be the only opportunity for your market to get a real sense of what working with you or using your product would be like, so stay away from offensive tactics.

My teleclasses are among my free tastes. They allow anyone to hear firsthand from me about my philosophies and consulting style. When they appreciate what they hear, they inquire about doing business with me. Off-limits would be a free recruiting booth at Women For Hire career expos or free tickets to Spark & Hustle events. Since those are services we sell, they don't qualify as a taste.

If you come up with a great, knock-my-socks-off taste offer, reach out to me at Facebook.com/Tory and tell me about it so I can send people your way.

Overcoming Objections

Most of us will do anything to avoid hearing no. No one likes rejection, but you can't be so afraid that it paralyzes you from moving ahead. As an entrepreneur, it's up to you to hunt every day. If you don't pick up the phone, have that conversation or ask for the business, who will?

If the sales process makes you cringe, learn to live with the discomfort. Accept that not everyone will want what you're offering and recognize that every accomplished business owner routinely encounters sales objections. The key to overcoming them is to perfect your pitch and learn what it takes to close the deal.

View sales objections as valuable tools: when a prospective customer balks, it's a chance to address the concern head-on and overcome it. Be ready to persuasively address sales objections related to your specific offering.

When I pitched my first Women For Hire event, the HR manager at a popular chain of upscale restaurants asked me if his company could attend the event for free until they evaluated the results. He argued that since I didn't have a track record, he wasn't willing to risk his recruiting budget on my unproven expo. My response: a firm no. I made two arguments: First, if I dined at any of his restaurants, I wouldn't have the option to pay or not pay the bill at the end of the meal. I'd get the bill whether or not I liked the food. More important, I told him, I was in this business for the long haul. He could take a chance to join me for the inaugural event, knowing that I'd be doing everything to ensure success so he'd be back again. Or he could skip it, wait for feedback from participants and then join us in the future. He registered that day.

Make it clear that you understand the sales objections. You're not going to argue your way into a sale. Never make your prospective clients defend their feedback. It will only solidify their objections. Instead let them know you understand their hesitation. For example, when they say, "Gee, this is so expensive." Instead of saying, "No it's not," you should say, "I understand the fee is an investment." Then carry on from there with the benefits and value.

A sales coach pitched himself to be a speaker at Spark & Hustle. He told me that if attendees followed his sales system, they'd *never* have to deal with rejections again. After listening to him, I politely *rejected* his offer. It's absurd to pretend that anyone is immune to hearing no.

Restate the objection to your client. Make sure you understand their hesitation or reluctance to buy. You also want to establish if that is the only objection to moving forward with the sale. Ask if there are any other objections. You don't want to address their pricing concerns, only to have buyers bring up other issues later in the conversation. Ask so that you understand all potential concerns up front.

Reframe the objection. Be ready to talk about what your product or service can do for the client. Suggest what the risk of not buying at this time could be. For example, let's say you're a business coach whose prospective client wants to make more money, but says she can't afford coaching services. You could reframe the objection by asking, "If you don't get help now, what is likely to change on your own that will enable you to generate more revenue, especially since you've been struggling with this for some time?"

Keep track of each no. If you continue to hear the same objections, they may be telling you more about your product or service than about your target market. Use a simple table or Excel document to keep track of the responses.

Be sure to note:

What is the objection?

_____

Can it be easily addressed?

_____

What does your prospect need to know in order to overcome the objection?

_____

What truth is behind the objection?

_____

How often does this objection come up?

_____

The responses may lead you to realize that you're targeting the wrong market. You may have to adjust your pitch, product, service, pricing or a combination of all four. Only by studying the nature of the objections can you make these tweaks, so don't bury your head on this stuff.

Follow up. This is the single most important step when you don't make a sale. Ask for permission to contact the prospect in the future to check in, and then be sure to do it. _No_ often means _not now_, so stay in a relationship with your prospects so that when they are ready to buy, you will be their first call.

When Liz Lange suggested to her then-boss that he launch a line of maternity wear to save his struggling fashion house, he rejected it, saying pregnant women wouldn't spend money on high-end clothing. Several top retailers also dismissed her idea. So she decided to go for it herself—taking individual appointments for made-to-order pieces. As she began dressing pregnant celebrities—a full decade before star bellies were all the rage in gossip magazines—business picked up and she soon landed a licensing deal with Nike for maternity active wear. The brand blossomed from there—thanks largely to her refusal to listen to the naysayers. Now she's not only a maternity master, but Liz is a true retail pioneer for challenging the assumptions about what women wanted.

Selling Not Pushing

When I discuss sales with women, they often worry that they'll seem pushy. Tierra Destiny Reid sold dozens of tickets to Spark & Hustle conferences. Cindy W. Morrison sold almost every seat at Tulsa's Spark & Hustle. As someone who has run a business based largely on events, I know that neither of these women succeeded without concerted effort. Not only did I not receive any complaints about their sales technique—nobody called them pushy, but many attendees raved about how grateful they were that Tierra and Cindy got them there.

Business and motivational gurus often say there's no such thing as a bad idea. They prove it in four words: "Teenage Mutant Ninja Turtles." Who would have guessed that a group of pizza-eating sewer turtles could gross more than $8 billion? Surely whatever you're selling can make it, too, if you have a solid sales strategy.

Is it possible to sell something you know is a sham or scam? Of course, but it will certainly make you feel poorer for it and at some point you'll be labeled a fraud. Tierra and Cindy both said that their job was easy because they believed in me and knew that Spark & Hustle could do for other women what it had done for them when they attended my first event in 2010.

Find your sweet spot, which likely lies at the intersection between what your prospective clients know they need and what your product or service can do for them. In other words, apply all you know about your product or service to all you know about the person you're selling to. If the person is on a supertight budget, mention your payment options. If the prospect is desperate for specific results, share testimonials along those lines. Tapping your sweet spot will result in sales that feel more authentic to you and your prospects.

Let's look at what will become your sales guidepost.

➤ Do you believe wholeheartedly in what you're selling? If the answer isn't yes, work on your product or service.

➤ Ditch boilerplate pitches and fancy marketing talk in favor of genuine conversation. List all the benefits of your product or service. What do you love most about it? Make sure that's in your pitch.

➤ Know your sweet spot. It may change for each niche or person, but write down all you know to be true about your product or service, and apply those points to all you know to be true about your prospect. That information is crucial to making the sale, especially when you're offering a pricy or personalized product or service. You may not nail this in a day, so keep at it until it feels just right. You won't know that for sure until you get into conversation.

Your Story Is Your Best Asset

You know my fired-to-hired story. What you may not know is that pretty much anytime I speak to a group of people about job-searching or career advancement, I share it. Why? Because it resonates with anyone who has ever worked in corporate America. Many have received a pink slip, some fear a layoff and everyone knows someone who's been fired.

Your story doesn't have to be as dramatic as mine to make it part of your sales process. But you should take time to answer the question of why you do what you do. Maybe you're like me: you had a passion for a specific niche and a burning desire for financial independence. Use your story to convince your prospect that buying from you is the best option and that you are the Real Deal.

Keep this in perspective. Don't share your story hoping to convert pity to cash: this is a chance to let others know who you are and what makes you tick. It's about leveraging the challenges, experiences and circumstances that have shaped who you are and how you're able to best serve others today. It infuses your business with an authenticity that will draw people in and effectively carve out a space for you.

Take a moment to consider your own path and how you got to where you are right now. How does your core story intersect with the work you do for clients? Write it down and review it to get comfortable making a natural connection.

Use Testimonials

Two things about testimonials:

1. What others say about you, your products and your services after experiencing the benefits firsthand may be more convincing than what you say about yourself, no matter how good you are at it.

2. Many business owners undervalue testimonials or don't use them effectively.

Strategically capturing and using testimonials can set you apart from your competitors. Testimonials:

➤ Increase sales by creating proof of what your product or service can do for your target market

➤ Eliminate the perceived risk of trying something new

➤ Keep the positive results of what you sell in front of your target market

➤ Expand exposure within your target market when used strategically within social media

➤ Lead to repeat buys from existing customers

➤ Inspire referrals—when your clients are asked to craft a testimonial for you, they actually re-sell themselves on your product or service

WHAT MAKES A GREAT TESTIMONIAL?

A common mistake that business owners make is posting ineffective testimonials on their websites or in marketing materials. Here are a few examples of seemingly "good" testimonials:

"Thanks so much for putting on the seminar yesterday. I loved meeting you and hearing what you had to say."

"Working with Allison was a real joy. She has a fantastic personality and we enjoyed working with her very much."

"I just bought my first car from Lisa. She was great and I'll definitely be back!"

At first glance, you might ask: What is wrong with any of them? That's probably because you've seen similar ones dozens of times.

But the truth is they all suck. They focus more on the personality of the seller than on the worth of what's being sold. Rather than collecting testimonials about what a great person you are, how easy it is to talk with you or how much the client enjoyed his or her session, seek testimonials that are specific and focus on results.

Here's one I got from a woman who attended one of my events: "Two weeks after attending the three-day program, I closed $9,800 in business from new clients. I credit the specific tactics I learned at the conference with enabling me to make this happen."

It's specific and results-oriented. You can read it once and see why it's so powerful. She doesn't waste time gushing about how much she enjoyed meeting me. That's irrelevant to my next prospect.

Effective testimonials along the lines of the latter two listed above might read:

> *"Allison is a results-driven consultant, capable of solving the most complex marketing issues. Within just three weeks, she helped us double our monthly revenue."*

> *"Lisa is an efficient, responsive saleswoman. Unlike most people in her position, she listened to our needs and didn't pressure us to spend a penny more than we'd budgeted. We were thrilled with the experience and we love our new car."*

CAPTURING TESTIMONIALS

Long before I opened the doors to attendees at my Spark & Hustle conferences, I spent a lot of time trying to ensure that they would not only produce a profit for me, but also lead to a healthy increase in income for attendees. After you've worked tirelessly to make your event, service or product praiseworthy, here's how to capture great testimonials:

Mail. When you get heartfelt thank-you notes from clients or customers, save them. Ask the sender for permission to scan and use a digital version as a testimonial on your website. If your business has a physical location, display the notes prominently.

PHOTOS. At a popular grocery store outside New York City called Stew Leonard's, customers save their plastic grocery bags. They send photos of themselves displaying the bags in remote places across the globe. Stew posts them on a bulletin board near the checkout lines and they never fail to draw my attention. Goofy, but this little gesture shows that Stew values every customer. It's a powerful testimonial to just how much shoppers love this store.

SPOKEN WORD. When you get great feedback from clients, ask if you can include it in a testimonial. Don't leave it to them to put it in writing, since most people won't. Instead, write it down and get their approval. Most people are happy for you to capture their words this way.

JUST ASK. If a testimonial isn't forthcoming, but you know someone is satisfied with your product or service, ask for one. Make this script your own: "I'm thrilled you like my work. I'd be honored if you'd consider providing me with a testimonial that I can use on my website and in my marketing materials. I'd be happy to draft it based on your initial comments to me, and then I'll send it for your approval since I want to be sure it accurately conveys how you feel and that you're comfortable with it."

You can also prompt great testimonials through a key question:

"What three specific changes did you experience
after using this product?"

"What are the three most tangible benefits you realized
after working with me?"

Along the same lines, look for opportunities to use something nice that someone has said about you. I was a guest on Dave Ramsey's radio show, and before I knew it, he was saying the most complimentary things about my work with entrepreneurs. It came out of the blue and coming from him, a beloved entrepreneurial guru and one of my business heroes, held enormous clout. So I posted a clip of his words on my website for potential Spark & Hustle attendees to hear.

SOCIAL MEDIA. If someone tweets or posts something nice about you, don't let it go to waste. Take a screen shot and use it on your website or in sales materials. Re-tweet and share it online, too.

BLOGS. Blogs are another great place to capture testimonials about you, your company or your products. Set up Google Alerts, which monitor websites and blogs in real time for references to specific people, products or companies, to capture any mention of you or your company. To do this, go to Google.com/alerts and enter your search terms and email address.

Selling in Prime Time

When my kids were in preschool at our local YMCA on the Upper West Side of Manhattan, they became friends with an adorable little boy named Michael, whose mom happened to be Kelly Ripa. The kids became friends and the moms became friends, too.

No doubt you've seen *Live!* so you know the show begins with fifteen minutes of host chat about everything from fashion to the weather to other happenings in the world and around New York.

So at one point very early in our friendship, I mentioned to Peter that I wanted to ask Kelly to talk about my upcoming career fair during that chitchat time. Great idea, he said. Then every week I sat with Kelly as our kids played. Every week, I practiced asking her. Every week, I chickened out. I kept convincing myself that "when the time was right," I would ask.

I was waiting for the perfect moment, something I couldn't define. What exact conditions constitute the right timing for anything? Birds chirping around my head, perhaps? Yet that's exactly what I hear from so many business owners who never ask for the sale or the testimonial. Waiting for the *right* time is the same thing as *wasting* time. There is *never* a perfect moment.

Men have this strategy down. I think most of them are born with it. They'll sell on the golf course, while working out, even at church or synagogue. They recognize the urgency involved in the selling process and have a "sell now" mentality. Women should take a page from their playbook.

There's no need to be obnoxious, pushy or inappropriate. Use tact, wisdom and even your intuition, particularly if you recognize yourself in my story. If you're waiting, putting the sales conversation off or just not making any sales moves at all, the urgency of "sell now" will serve you well.

Incidentally, I finally approached Kelly and asked for her help, only after Peter caught me rehearsing my pitch to her for the umpteenth time like a big shot in front of the mirror and threatened to ask her for me if I didn't just do it.

But I made the mistake with Kelly of starting out with disclaimers. "I have to ask you something, and I hope you don't think I'm using you. I hope you're not going to be mad at me. It's OK if you want to say 'no.'"

You'd think I was asking this woman if I could borrow $1 million, weakening my request before I even got to it.

Fortunately, Kelly told me to spit it out. I explained that I was hosting a free event for women job-seekers in New York, and I was hoping she might be willing to give it a little plug. I said I knew she was always supportive of working women, and this event complemented her other efforts. Her response: "That sounds terrific—what a great service. I'd be happy to promote it." And the next day she did just that.

HOW TO ASK FOR A PLUG

Start out strong and stay positive: "I have a favor to ask and I'm hoping you'll say yes." Then explain the nature of the request. Be ready to offer a clear explanation of why this is a natural fit for the person's time or talent. If you sense hesitation or discomfort, suggest that the person think about it for a day or two before responding. Offer to answer any questions, or provide additional clarification to make it easier for him or her.

Once someone agrees to your request, ask what you can do to help facilitate it. With Kelly, I offered to provide three bullet points about the event on a note card so she had the key information handy. The easier you can make it, the better.

Always thank someone, whether or not the person does what you asked. A verbal or email "thanks for considering my request" is sufficient if you were denied. And a handwritten note or even a small gift is appropriate if the request was fulfilled. After she spoke about Women For Hire on air, I asked Kelly's assistant for her favorite florist and I sent a huge arrangement as a token of my appreciation.

You can do this, too. You have high-profile or influential people like Kelly in your community, people with clout who can help you and impact your bottom line. Figure out how to connect with them in person, by phone or email. This may be clergy, a CEO, a school principal, a civic leader or any number of people. Only when you're willing to speak up and ask for help or for the sale will you be able to grow your business. Nobody else will do it for you.

act now

- Always sell yourself first.

- Banish fancy marketing talk and brochure-speak. Create authentic conversations instead.

- Make a Top 50 prospect list and add to it regularly.

- Use taste tests to help sell your product or service.

- Prepare to overcome objections to your pitch.

- Use your own story to sell your product or service.

- Leverage testimonials.

- No hinting. Ask directly for the sale.

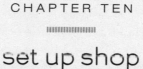

set up shop

Many women set up shop before conducting any real business planning or strategy. They waste money on unnecessary legal and accounting fees that could have been better used in other places. They declare a legal business structure and open a bank account before they're ready to launch, market or grow. They get so excited about the idea of having a business that they jump the gun.

Most fail. I don't want you to be one of them.

But now you're ready. You have everything you need to make your business a reality. Time to decide which legal structure your business will take.

You likely have three basic choices:

➤ Sole proprietorship

➤ Legal partnership

➤ Corporation

HIRE WISELY

You are who you hire, says Paige Arnof-Fenn, who owns Mavens & Moguls (mavensandmoguls.com), a Cambridge, Massachusetts, firm that helps companies with branding, PR and market research. "Make sure everyone represents you well," she says. "Even if you are a good judge of character, you can get burned. When it is your company, you are the brand: everyone you bring in is a reflection of your business."

Consider this an overview of your options, with basic advantages and disadvantages of each. Speak to a lawyer, an accountant—or both—before making your decision. Skimping on legal and accounting issues by using a cheap service provider or do-it-yourself options could hurt you in the long run. Buy the very best professional advice you can afford. It's worth it.

Sole Proprietorship

The most popular legal structure for small businesses is a sole proprietorship. This is basically a way to launch your small business as an extension of yourself, without extra legal formalities. It's probably the most popular business structure because it's the easiest. The only legal requirements may be applying for a business license within your local city or county jurisdiction. If your business name is anything other than your given legal name, you'll also need to file a DBA (doing business as) statement, which allows you to open a business checking account under your business name. In some areas, a DBA is also called a "fictitious business name" or "trade name."

Besides being easy and inexpensive, a sole proprietorship offers other advantages. You have complete control over the business, and other than your own personal tax return, there's no additional income tax filing required.

But freedom and ease come with a price. Establishing your business as a sole proprietorship means that you are personally liable for all business debts, which are not limited to the value of the business itself. You'll also find it more difficult to secure start-up funding through traditional lenders for your business as a sole proprietor.

Legal Partnership

As the name implies, a partnership means that you and at least one other person own the business. Each partner shares in the operation as well as the profits, debts and liabilities. Some advantages include having a partner whose skills, expertise and spheres of influence complement or exceed yours. Having two minds instead of one can be a plus. You can pool your personal resources for start-up funds and work together to get the business off the ground.

But forming a legal partnership can be messy if the two of you

KNOW IT ALL

Shameeka Ayers is the Broke Socialite (thebrokesocialite.com), her alter ego, who produces lifestyle tours (think bakery crawls) with a social media twist. Entrepreneurs need to own every detail, she says. "Everyone doesn't have your best interest at heart. Regardless of who I hire, I need to know every aspect of my business in case I must step in for a contractor, vendor, intern or employee."

aren't on the same page. Another disadvantage is that you may be liable for any of your partner's financial commitments, personal or otherwise. That can get sticky. And aside from the legal and financial ramifications of a business partnership going south, you also risk ruining a great personal friendship. So tread lightly before you ask your best pal to become your partner. If you go this route, agree in writing on how you'd dissolve the partnership without destroying the business if you have a falling out.

ALWAYS ALWAYS

Always have an attorney review any legal document, says Lisa Johnson of Modern Pilates (modernpilatesboston.com), a Brookline, Massacusetts, studio. "I trusted a landlord and just signed a lease without having a lawyer look it over. That was a big mistake that I had to live with for years—and painfully expensive."

Corporation

To minimize personal liability, many people choose to establish their business as a corporation, which allows you to create a complex legal entity separate from your personal finances. While your personal liability is not as vulnerable with this structure, your record keeping, tax burden and government oversight increase, so get good legal and accounting advice before incorporating. In addition to limited legal and financial liability, advantages here include an ability to raise traditional funding if you need it.

Keeping It Legal

Every town, county, city and state has its own laws governing businesses. Regardless of where you live, you can visit score.org or your local chamber of commerce for information on local laws and business requirements. Business bankers also tend to know legal requirements in their area.

If you are operating your business as a corporation or partnership or you have employees, you'll have to apply for an employer ID number (EIN), which you can do online through irs.gov. It's a quick and simple process.

Your Business Checking Account

Regardless of the business structure you choose, open a business checking account. I know many business owners are tempted to skip this step, especially home-based business owners and freelancers doing business under their own name and Social Security number, but it's best to keep your personal finances separate from your business finances, especially if you're committed to growing this venture. It makes keeping tabs on your income, expenses, pricing and taxes much easier.

Legally Hiring Free Help

The entrepreneurial creed is to do more with less, cut corners where you can and maximize every opportunity available to you. That's why very few things are as tempting for the hustling, driven business owner as getting free help, also known as an intern. But you need to do it right to avoid getting into trouble with the U.S. Labor Department.

SMALL CAN BE GREAT

Laurie Baggett, of Chesapeake, Virginia, is a consultant who helps entrepreneurial-minded physicians expand their earnings and market themselves effectively. "I don't want to bring on and manage employees to increase my client base," she says. "So I intentionally keep my business simple and exclusive."

Make sure that the intern opportunity you're creating meets very specific criteria set forth by the government. Your goal may be to get free help, but Uncle Sam says internships must clearly benefit your trainees—especially if you're not paying them.

SurePayroll.com, which provides online payroll services to small businesses, including mine, advises clients that an internship should give participants "valuable work experience that will leave them better-prepared to become professionals." This means that you'll have to design your internship offer or program in such a way that:

➤ The experience is similar to the hands-on training provided in a vocational or academic institution.

➤ Trainees do not displace regular employees.

➤ You can provide the time and intellectual investment necessary to give the trainee a valuable experience.

➤ Trainees are not promised a job at the conclusion of the training.

➤ Interns understand that it is an unpaid position.

As new laws continue to develop governing these situations, check with www.dol.gov/whd/flsa and your state laws before making a move.

Let's assume you're in the clear. You've got some great projects lined up and can provide an intern with a valuable experience, and the situation you've created is legal, according to the Fair Labor Standards Act. Now how do you find your intern?

Start by contacting career services offices at your local college or university. Identify clubs on campus that relate to your business objective. LinkedIn is a great place to find interns. Since it's a professional setting, you often get more targeted responses than you'll get from Craigslist, which can also be a place to post your opening.

When you find star interns, nurture them. Check in regularly and encourage them. Set clear expectations and boundaries. Give candid feedback. Most successful people I've met can vividly recall an internship that set them on their path to glory.

After she graduated from the University of Michigan and moved to New York, Alex Hall joined Women For Hire as an intern. She was eager to learn and wanted to contribute to everything we were working on. As a result she wound up doing more than some of our employees at the time. She was clearly the best

STAYING SAFE

Kim Pollard, who owns Bookkeeper Girl (bookkeepergirl.com), which provides online bookkeeping and payroll services to small business owners, says you should keep some aspects of your business private. Having the same online login as your bookkeeper "can be dangerous. Never share your personal login or security questions with anyone. Always have at least one that nobody knows."

intern I'd ever had, so I made her an offer to stay on full-time. Everyone who attends a Spark & Hustle event gets to know Alex quite well. She's an integral part of the growth of the company and I couldn't imagine doing any of this without her.

Common Legal Pitfalls for Small Business Owners

Regardless of your business structure or number of employees, be aware of common pitfalls that could cost you dearly. Even if you work alone, set up your business to protect you.

I often turn to SurePayroll for advice in this area. I'll include some of the most relevant tips here, and you can get much more at SurePayroll.com. As with any other legal or tax issue, use this information as a guide, but follow the advice of an attorney or accountant who knows your specific needs.

PITFALL # 1: Not getting your employer ID number. If you are hiring another person, even part-time or on a temporary basis, you need an employer ID number from the Department of Labor.

PITFALL # 2: Not reporting new hires. Most business owners do not even know that they must report new hires to their state labor department, and they pay anywhere from $25 to $500 in penalty fees for each employee unreported.

PITFALL # 3: Misclassifying workers. State and federal governments are cracking down on this, as many small business owners (sole proprietors as well) are paying workers as independent contractors when they're basically full-time and more accurately "employees." There are complex classification criteria for anyone you pay to provide a service. Misclassifying employees as contractors can cost you up to $25,000 per employee, plus back taxes and interest.

PITFALL #4: Not understanding employee deductions and tax responsibilities. Nothing puts a damper on your moneymaking abilities like having the IRS hit you with penalties and back taxes. Do not mess with this. Seek proper advice and consider using a professional payroll service to handle such issues for you.

BE CAREFUL

It doesn't matter how good you are at what you do if the people around you are incompetent, says Carolyn Rowley of Cayenne Wellness Center (cayennewellness.org), a Glendale, California, organization dedicated to patients' mental, physical and spiritual health. She says hire wisely. "Your staff can harm your business if you aren't careful."

Aside from legal pitfalls, there are other potential dangers to consider when making hiring decisions. This is true for interns, freelancers and full-time staff. When I made my initial hires, I chose employees I wanted as friends. I figured I trusted them with my baby, so it was important to like them personally. That was a disaster. It works when you need a shopping pal or someone to see a movie with—not when you're tackling business. So I went the opposite route: I hired people whom I wouldn't even want to have lunch with, people with skills to just do the job, period. Another bust. Here I was running a company that was all about hiring great talent, yet I couldn't do it myself. Trust me, the irony of that was not lost on me.

In the end, just as I lean on accountants and lawyers for their expertise, I now ask for help from people who know all about recruiting and hiring. They review my job descriptions, screen candidates and talk me through each finalist before I extend an offer.

When you're ready to build a team, seek advice from someone who has managed people and can offer you insights based on your needs. You can ask me, too, at Facebook.com/Tory. I think I finally have a handle on this hiring thing.

Remember, even if you work alone, your first employee is you. Spend the necessary time and money to ensure that you've set up your business properly.

act now

- A business owner will typically set up shop before ever conducting any real business planning or strategy. A logo and bank account don't make a business.

- Determine your business structure by seeking professional advice that's catered specifically to your needs and goals.

- Visit score.org and your local chamber of commerce to learn about local laws and business requirements.

- Keep your business income and personal income separate.

- Retain the services of qualified professionals who can handle the legal stuff that you're not qualified to address.

- Understand the law governing internships if you decide to seek free labor.

||||||||||||||||||||

CHAPTER ELEVEN

hustle every day

So you've been hustling for a while, yet you're coming up short of your goals, despite your best efforts. In your mind you're doing everything right, doing everything possible to succeed, yet your product or service is not selling. It does no good to blame the economy for these troubles, and it's definitely not a sign that it's time to pack up your tent and admit defeat.

Instead, look at ways to troubleshoot your business: What have you done wrong or not done at all?

First, make sure your brand, product or service aligns with the audience you're talking to. If I sell high-end women's shoes and talk them up at an event for struggling single dads and leave without a single sale, does that mean my product or business stinks? Of course not. It simply means I'm talking to the wrong people about what I offer. If you're struggling with sales, assess whether you're connecting with the right audience.

Second, look at your pricing and the perceived value of what you're charging. Lack of sales doesn't necessarily mean it's time to lower prices. In some cases the opposite is true: clients look at your cheap fees and assume you're no good. At such a low cost, they may assume what you're selling isn't up to par.

Years ago for our side business, Peter and I scoured English country flea markets then returned home to sell antiques at small, upscale weekend shows. He priced our merchandise to sell— knowing that we had paid very little. Peter had a Walmart mentality: price it low, they will come, and the volume will be grand. But it didn't work because in the antiques world, many buyers expect high prices because to them, hefty price tags indicate that the merchandise is authentic, unique and worth buying. To them, the very low priced stuff—no matter how interesting—is probably a reproduction or junk. So we changed gears by putting fancy tags and high prices on our flea market finds and sold a bundle.

We took anything we didn't sell to less expensive flea markets and priced it to sell, which it did. In both cases, we aligned ourselves with our customers.

If you're unsure about how to price your product or service, redo your marketing study: ask a fresh group of people in your target audience what they would pay for your service or product, then price based on what they tell you—assuming it covers your costs and allows for profit. If that price doesn't cover costs and allow a profit, rethink your hard costs and profit expectations. You may need to tinker with one or both.

Third, are you shouting at clients or engaging them in real conversations? Are you blasting a lot of stuff *at* them or talking *with* them?

When she founded 600 lb. Gorillas, Inc., a frozen cookie dough business, Paula White of Duxbury. Massachusetts, spent thousands of dollars on billboards, radio and TV ads—you name it—to get her company name out there. Her phone didn't ring. So Paula began a grassroots campaign: she approached food buyers at trade shows, handed out samples in stores and talked directly to shoppers. All of that one-on-one chatter got the fledgling business off the ground. It's now a multimillion-dollar nationwide enterprise.

Along the same lines, in the early days of SurePayroll, president Michael Alter bought an expensive email list, having been assured that people on the list were the perfect target market for his new payroll service. Michael and his team were so confident about the anticipated results of this email campaign that they set up extra phone lines and customer service operators to handle the flood of likely calls.

The phone never rang—and Michael realized that SurePayroll had zero brand recognition. No one knew anything about this new service, which meant they weren't going to sign up for it based on a single email blast. Michael decided that before he could sell it, he needed to educate prospects about SurePayroll. With a variety of bigger payroll services to choose from, he had to explain in detail why it was in anyone's best interest to switch. Today, SurePayroll is the online payroll company of choice for small businesses.

Last, you've done a great job getting people interested in you, but you're still struggling when it comes to converting interest into sales. Tackle this with a simple question to yourself: are you *asking* for the sale or merely *hinting* at it? Many of us find it difficult to ask directly for the sale, which leaves opportunity and money on the table. Force yourself to *ask* for the sale. Practice your pitch, so you enter into any sales conversation brimming with confidence. If you're not willing to put yourself out there to sell your product or service, why should any customer buy it?

At some of our Spark & Hustle conferences, one of our popular exercises is nicknamed "Spark Tank"—a takeoff on TV's *Shark Tank*. We give attendees thirty seconds to stand in front of everyone and pitch what they do. (Alex has a stopwatch and rings a little bell if anyone goes over the time limit.) Then, a panel candidly critiques them.

Some women nail it—and earn loud applause. Others stumble—but glean valuable advice from the judges on how to pump up their presentation. If you have doubts about the effectiveness of your pitch, test it in front of people you can trust to be candid—then pay attention to their feedback.

The hard truth is you may never feel comfortable asking for the sale. You can read every sales book, take endless sales courses, get extensive sales coaching, practice on end, yet it may never come easily, no matter how much you try. In that case, learn to live with the discomfort; otherwise no sales means no business. If you want this business to take off, you'll ask for the sale even if you don't like doing so.

Another issue is time. Saying you don't have enough of it is often a lame excuse for not getting things done. Think of the most successful people you know—the President, Oprah, any business leader—and you'll realize the one thing you have in common is twenty-four hours in a day. Nobody has more—making effective time management the best kept secret of the world's wealthiest and most successful people. How you spend your workday is directly tied to how successful you'll be in business. I've identified strategies that make a measurable difference in my life and income. They can do the same for you if you implement them consistently.

Beware of Information Overload

We all want to be in the know, but you can drown in information, surfing the Web and wasting valuable time when your business needs you. Information guzzling is passive. To fight it, be proactive. Read in the tub or surf the net at night when the kids are asleep. Don't get lost in checking out photos of Facebook friends throughout the day. During office hours, concentrate on tasks that *make you money.*

THE GUILT GAME

When you're eager to please everyone while managing dozens of responsibilities, it's all about choices. "Should you leave your family to go on a business trip that could potentially land you a new client," asks Beth Feldman, founder of RoleMommy.com. "If it means you won't miss your son's championship game or daughter's recital, then go for it. Be present as a mom as you build your empire and your family will cheer you on every step of the way."

Plan Your Brainstorms

As a rule, women entrepreneurs are a creative bunch. But there are times when we're so flush with new ideas that they get in the way of actual work. You can't afford to dilute your time, attention and energy constantly thinking about new ideas that may or may not work. Instead, write down all those ideas and put them in a folder. Once a week, each month or every quarter, get out the folder and review them with the benefit of time. You may find that some don't hold up.

Beat Procrastination

Procrastination costs you time, money and unnecessary stress. Most of us typically procrastinate on things we anticipate will be a pain in the neck. Start your day by tackling the hardest stuff before you check your email or make a call.

Commit to a Schedule

I'm old-fashioned and still prefer a paper calendar to manage my schedule—despite all the fancy online calendars and apps available. I don't "fit in" anything important. I schedule it. I don't put it on a "to do" list. I assign it and give myself realistic deadlines. I also build in time for the unexpected, which is especially important when you're managing multiple priorities. For me, that includes family, my TV duties and projects outside my day-to-day businesses. When I get a last-minute call to appear on TV, which requires prep time, I don't let it ruin my day, because I have a built-in buffer for unplanned requests.

Micromanage Your Time

While writing this book, I didn't just schedule one big block of time for writing. I scheduled specific time to write each chapter. The more specific your schedule, the more focused you are. Breaking down tasks will make large projects feel less daunting.

Daily 5 x 5 Plan

Focus on a daily 5 × 5 plan—five things to do by 5 P.M. every day to meet your business goals. This list may consist of making specific sales calls, reaching out to media contacts, scheduling networking conversations, engaging in social media, checking on vendor deadlines—doing whatever is necessary to bring in sales. The best 5 × 5 plan is one where all five tasks are measurable and impact business growth. Stay away from putting income-neutral tasks like bookkeeping and filing on your list. While those things must get done, too, focus on them after hours.

BIG PICTURE FOCUS

"Focus on the big picture by asking, what activity drives or grows my business," says Gretchen Gunn of MGD Services (mgdservices.com), a staffing firm based in New Jersey. "Be careful not to get lost in the minutiae of daily tasks at the expense of focusing on profit-producing activities. If something is going to take a lot of time and yet it's not directly related to generating revenue, my preference is to delegate the task. When that's not possible, I handle it after-hours."

Email or Not?

Email is without a doubt my biggest time-sucker. I could preach about never starting your day by opening your inbox, since it will wind up creating a "to do" list for you and driving your day's agenda. I could suggest that you check your email just three times a day. I could warn you about the dangers of allowing email to take over your life.

But I'd be a hypocrite.

I am glued to email—both at my desk and on the go. I can barely sit through a two-hour movie without checking my Black-Berry. It drives my kids nuts at dinnertime when I check messages at the table. Peter sometimes asks on long road trips if I plan to talk to him at all during the ride. Rude, maybe, but it works for me.

I've become pretty efficient when managing email. I try to deal with each one once, which means I read an email and then respond, delete, delegate or file it. I'm more relaxed when I can handle things as they come my way. This often surprises people who email me. They're stunned that it's really me answering—and usually very quickly—at many hours of the day and night.

Figure out what's best for you.

What Will You Do Today?

I end every Spark & Hustle conference by asking attendees a simple question: "How many of you are going back home to a perfect business incubator, the one with no partner, no kids, no health concerns, no outside distractions, just you and your business?"

No one ever raises her hand.

I want women who attend my events—whether they have strong and established businesses or are just starting out—to use what they've learned *immediately*. It's not enough that you attended, took notes and had a great time. It's what you do when you get home that separates the successes and strugglers.

It's what you do every day, what you accomplish, that will differentiate you from other business owners. To achieve your magic number, you must take deliberate and disciplined steps to get there. It's all about the hustle—the decisions you make and the actions you take.

Evaluate how you spend your time:

How am I proactively planning the week ahead?

_____

Am I usually putting out fires or fueling my financial growth?

_____

What profit-producing actions am I taking now?

_____

Which actions do I know for sure bring in the most money for my business?

_____

What three things could I do right now to make my schedule more productive?

_____

Sometimes just putting it in black-and-white helps you focus.

Dealing with Distractions When Working from Home

As in any workplace, there are plenty of distractions to overcome if you work from home. Only at home, there's no one watching you to say, "Hey, get back to work." Get accustomed to your small business work environment.

Certain distractions may not stop you from working but can impair your professionalism or performance. If the dog barks every time someone walks or drives down the street and you're on important calls, something must change. If your office is knee-high with magazines and stacks of bills, you won't be as efficient as you could be in an orderly space.

It's all about discipline, boundaries and finding the right balance. Consider the woman who starts a home-based business because she has young children and an aging mom to look after. Because they are key priorities, she may not see them as distractions. But attending to their routine needs during her designated work hours is no smarter than sneaking out to see what's on sale at her favorite store when she should be working. It's very hard to work toward accomplishments when you don't give yourself uninterrupted time.

A few tips to minimize distractions:

Your home business should not double as a nursery or nursing home. You can't work while you watch your kids or other loved ones. The combination is counterproductive and chaotic. That means you should work while they're at school or day care or bring someone in to help—in another part of the house—while you work.

Build in breaks and stick to them. Women who work outside

their home have a commute, meetings, breaks, lunch and pop-in visits from coworkers. But women who work from home face long days—and some overwork themselves as a result. Others have trouble getting motivated and start watching TV, doing chores or hanging out on the Web. As a result, they have to *steal* time from family to make up the work. That defeats one of the main purposes that many women have chosen to work from home: to have more time with family.

If you work at home, create your own work flow, breaks and rewards. Set your schedule and rules at the beginning of the day or week and stick to them. For example, a daily walk at noon. No laundry or emptying the dishwasher until the afternoon break at 2:15 P.M. No work between 6:30 P.M. and 10 P.M. Soon enough you'll become an expert at honoring your work hours.

Hang it up. The phone is a huge distraction. As long as important people such as your kids' caretakers and schools have your work number, don't answer your home phone during work time. The minute you do, you're hemorrhaging time. Time that is money.

Clarify the rules. You can't expect your spouse, partner or kids to instantly respect your work time and space just because you've declared yourself in business. Establish signals with your family to let them know when you'll be working.

Occasionally inviting older kids to help as your assistant for an hour or two a week is a good way to engage the family. You could even offer compensation if they're interested.

With spouses or partners, it's a little tougher. Some women say their husbands or partners want to be part of the process, but when they don't really know how or what they should do, they may get angry or jealous. First, establish clearly that your husband or partner really does want to be part of your business, then

AVOID "SUPER MOM SYNDROME"

Pam Guyer, founder of HiPP MoMs (hippmoms.com), started her at-home business just after the birth of her third child. Pam coaches other women to balance family, home and work and to accept that no mom needs to be "Super Mom." She believes you can't do it all, but you can have it all by creating balance and prioritizing how you spend your time and energy. She encourages women to design their lives and select their priorities based on what's most important to them as individuals and what they deem most desirable. You can do the same.

find the logical place for such involvement. Is your partner creative? If so, designing e-flyers announcing your new venture may be a great task. Keep communication channels open since it may require some give-and-take to get it right.

The Week Ahead

One way to merge the action plan you've created with your calendar is to plan your week, every week. Doing so allows you to greet each Monday morning with a plan of action that won't be easily derailed and that allows you to accomplish more in less time. Sunday evening is a good time to hold your weekly planning meeting with yourself.

Schedule to-do items with an actual appointment time during which they will be completed. This is much different than simply making a list of items to check off. Increase efficiency by giving each action step a specific allotted time and a deadline.

Build in two thirty-minute blocks of time each day, one in the morning and one in the evening, to deal with unexpected issues as they arise, while staying on track with the rest of your schedule.

DON'T GO IT ALONE

You don't have to go it alone, says Angie Nelson, who owns ASN Virtual Services (asnvirtualservices.com) in Craig, Nebraska, which provides virtual services and blog consulting for online business owners. "I am a shy, private person. I had to get out of my shell, meet other women entrepreneurs and share my story. Now I have a strong, supportive network. There are other women facing the same struggles."

Schedule the most important item for the beginning of the day. These things tend to be the most time-consuming or require the most focus. Knock them out first. This can set the tone for productivity the rest of the day. You'll love yourself for completing the pain-in-the-butt stuff early on.

Hold Your Time Accountable for Producing Results

If your days are slipping by, take a look at how you're currently spending your work hours. Track your time the same way a nutritionist would ask you to track your diet: by writing down every bite. Focus on a single workweek: every activity, event (including travel time to and from), diversion, errand and conversation. You'll be able to see, quite clearly, where you are productive and where you need to be more efficient. Consider a simple time-tracker form like this one:

This form allows you to track your time, declare goals and

time in	time out	client / prospective client / goal	productive or not?
8:00	8:30	Social media networking— responding to questions on Twitter and Facebook about upcoming event	Yes—two new tickets sold
8:30	11:20	Networking meeting, including travel to and from, hoping to secure new clients	No—I've been attending weekly since January, and have received no new business as a result
11:25	12:30	Conversation with new client	Yes—delivering promised service

desired outcomes for how you're spending time and assess whether the time was productive. Fill in the time, activities and goals in real time and reflect at the end of each day on whether the time spent was productive. After one week of tracking, you'll have an eye-opening view of how well your schedule is aligned with your goals. You'll also have an idea of what must change and which distractions must go.

AVOID BURNOUT

Joanne Verkuilen owns Circle + Bloom (circlebloom.com), which creates mind-body audio programs to help women with their health and well-being. Her advice to entrepreneurs: take care of yourself. "You cannot build a business if you are empty, emotionally and physically. You will burn out."

Don't forget to schedule downtime. Your best ideas may come to you outside the office, when you're doing something fun. I do small things every week, like get a manicure. I take frequent walks in the park with my kids and our dog. I spend summer weekends outside the city. Our family gets away for an extended time at least twice a year. Many of my most profitable ideas have been generated during these moments—far away from the daily chaos of office.

No Excuses, Just Results

Your excuses are bullshit. I wish I could take credit for these terrific four words of advice, but they came from take-no-prisoners advice guru Mel Robbins at a New York Spark & Hustle event.

"Your excuses just make you feel safe," Mel is fond of saying. "Your mind wants you to do one thing: stay the course. The ones who make it are those who push themselves when they just don't feel like it."

There have been many times in the past thirteen years when I just "haven't felt like" working entire weekends or answering emails from women past midnight from my bed. I do it because I know that in order to grow my business I must put in the time. That's my choice.

In Tulsa, my entire Spark & Hustle weekend was threatened by a hotel staff that was paralyzed by below-freezing temperatures and a blanket of snow in a place that rarely gets a flake. No lobby heat, no hot water and delayed food deliveries—the staff shrugged their shoulders: "There's nothing we can do."

But what was I supposed to do, tell my attendees "Sorry"?

There's *always* something that can be done. There's *always* a

nurturing your mind, body and busine$$

You may often find yourself burning the candle at both ends, bogged down by problems and finding it hard to make good decisions on a consistent basis. You wrap up each week totally exhausted.

This was the pattern I followed for years, assuming there were no alternatives. Then I met three Spark & Hustle clients, each of whom practice and preach self-care. Even though they come to me for advice on how to build their brands and expand their services, they teach me a lot.

Pick and choose what works for you, and commit to incorporating some practices into your daily routine. It may take some getting used to, but self-care becomes second nature after a few weeks, especially as you begin to experience the results.

Lisa Briggs of IntuitiveBody.com recommends taking a few moments each morning to visualize the kind of day you want and need. Some days will be more action-oriented, while others are more quiet and nurturing. The choice is yours. Also, rather than writing a typical journal or diary, Lisa favors what she calls "journal purge." This is a form of therapeutic writing where you move out all of your negative energy by putting it on paper, releasing it and freeing up your thoughts.

Affirmations, when recited often, can help set the tone for how you'll mentally tackle the day. Among some of my top picks:

- "I'm worthy of the happiness that I will attract today."
- "Today I'll be mindful of my own well-being as I work to bring joy to others."
- "I know my possibilities for greatness are endless."

- "Nothing will prevent me from living today to my greatest potential."

Rosie Battista of CookingNakedAfter40.com honors her personal affirmations by making little beaded bracelets with words that provide strength in times of need. One of her favorites reads simply, "Bulletproof." Visit any craft store to pick up the supplies to create a unique visual reminder for your wrist.

Yoga is one of the most common and effective forms of self-care, and it's the relaxation method of choice for Melanie McGhee of PeaceFruit.com. She practices at least five times a week, and when she misses a day, she says her body begins to crave it. She recommends two poses—shavasana (the "corpse pose") and viparita karani, which involves lying perpendicular to a wall with your legs up on the wall. (Google them for step-by-step instructions.) Melanie says yoga always brings her back to a state of peace.

There's no right or wrong when it comes to self-care. The key is to find what works for you. What is good for your body is good for your mind—and good for your business.

way to overcome problems. So I lit a fire under that staff's butt and called the hotel chain's corporate office across the country to plead for backup. Everyone snapped into action and we pulled off the event.

Never give in. Never accept defeat.

Opportunity Overload

My hope is that you're inspired to take bold, strategic steps to make your dream of small business success a reality. One step is knowing when to say yes and no. Every yes comes with a no. When you spend money here, it's no longer available to spend elsewhere. This same concept applies to your time. For every thirty minutes you commit to proofreading a résumé for free, you're taking thirty minutes away from making money. An isolated incident won't hurt, but rarely are these choices the exception.

Ask yourself, "Will saying yes bring me measurably closer to my goals?" It's not always easy to tell at first. You may find yourself saying, "Well, it hasn't paid off yet, but . . ." Stay away from "yes, but . . ." thinking. Sure, not everything will have an immediate payoff—that's natural—but when that becomes the norm instead of the exception, it's time to rethink your schedule. Overall, if it doesn't get you closer to where you want to be—and you're not making the money you need—it's not worth your time right now.

THE REALITY OF TIME AND MONEY

Owning a business comes with flexibility, but it's not without a heavy workload, says Shannon Wilburn, founder of Just Between Friends Franchise Systems, Inc. (jbfsale.com), a national children's and maternity consignment sales event. "Most people have a basic assumption that business owners make a lot of money and have a lot of free time," but not so, says Shannon, who works much longer hours than she would as an employee on someone else's payroll. Get used to that if your financial goals are significant.

Done Is Good Enough

Done! That's the one-word response I love to hear from clients, staff and business partners. I have no doubt that attendees at my conferences find some small detail that I overlooked or a link on my website that doesn't work. While I want everything to be perfect, I've come to learn that "Done!" is usually *good enough*.

FLIP IT

When you're stuck or stalled, "Flip it. Look oppositely at everything you are doing," says Melody Biringer, founder of small business group, CRAVE (thecravecompany.com). "You may change everything or just tweak one thing, but looking at your project or business this way gets really interesting."

I've lost track of the number of clients who never posted their sales pages because the format wasn't perfect, didn't publish books because they couldn't stop fiddling with their manuscript, never had any sales conversations because the time wasn't "just right."

While others in my industry fuss over perfection, I'm talking, selling services and helping small business owners across the country. I'm not lowering my standards or justifying mediocre or sloppy work. But I have trained myself to make "Done!" a valid option.

Remember how I hemmed and hawed about reaching out to Kelly Ripa for a plug on *Live!*? What I was doing—in a nutshell— was waiting for the moon and the stars to align, for the heavenly choirs to begin singing, for the moment to be *just right* to approach her. When I finally took the plunge and forced myself to ask Kelly for the favor, I discovered that while not perfect, the moment was *good enough*. And I could say, "Done!"

Figure out the areas where your quest for perfection holds you back. Maybe you only put out a monthly newsletter because you spend so much time tweaking it. As a result, the specter of a weekly newsletter becomes overwhelming. Maybe you have put off launching your website for months because you're constantly coming up with new ideas to make it better. Perhaps you avoid going after a big fish because you think everything has to be flawless before you make that initial contact.

Write down the goal and then write down exactly what's standing in the way of making it happen. Is there any room for you to say this is "good enough" and move forward? Once you answer, consider it a marching order. There will always be time to improve on your initial sketch, newsletter, proposal or product. But waiting for perfection is a waste of time.

DECIDE FAST, ACT FASTER

Vicki Donlan (vickidonlan.com) is a business coach who works with entrepreneurs in the start-up, growth and exit phases of their businesses. She says men are better at taking direction than women. "They follow up better and they make decisions faster. Women tend to have many more excuses for why they don't do what they say they will do."

Pounce, Pause, or Pass?

I hate missed opportunities. When you dive into small business, you're surrounded by opportunity. You'll have to train yourself to pounce on the right opportunities and turn away the wrong ones.

In my office, we have a Pounce List that we always act on immediately. For instance, when a woman who attends a Women For Hire career expo mentions that the company her sister works for should be a part of our next event, we pounce. We ask for the sister's name and reach out to get her company for our next career expo. The same is true when small business owners come to me at Spark & Hustle events and say they wish they could "bottle my advice" or have more access to me during a specific phase of their business growth. Instead of just smiling politely and accepting the compliment, I share brief details of how we can work together.

Far too many business owners think of pouncing as something to be done only when huge opportunities present themselves. Opportunities to pounce usually surface every day, so keep your own key pounce list top of mind.

On the flip side, sometimes pouncing too soon is a bad idea. I'm pretty good at judging whether a proposal or idea is wrong for me, and if it is, I say no right away. But sometimes I lie awake at night thinking of ideas, or my staff comes up with something good, and I'm tempted to pounce on it immediately. (Remember my brilliant T-shirt idea?) So on ideas that ostensibly look terrific I've trained myself to sit for forty-eight hours before I commit. I've learned that if it was brilliant on Wednesday, it'll still be genius on Friday. But many ideas don't survive the forty-eight-hour rule.

Set parameters for when to pounce immediately and when to pause before deciding to pass or proceed.

NO

Jennifer Lee, a success coach (coachjennlee.com) and Florida native, gets right to the heart of what holds too many women back from success: overcommitment. "No is a complete sentence." Be confident of that.

NO MORE NINE-TO-FIVE

Nine-to-five is for sissies, says Beth Anderson, who runs Chic Galleria Publications (chicgalleria.com) in Tulsa, Oklahoma, which publishes an online fashion and lifestyle magazine and offers blog copy and editing services. "Don't always expect to be contacted during normal business hours," she says. "I hear from clients every day of the week, at all hours of the day and night. I'm ready for them."

Change As Needed

It takes time to get any business going. There's something to be said for persistence and perseverance, but they're only profitable if you're doing the right things, with the right market, at the right time. It's dangerous to continue doggedly in the face of overwhelming evidence that you should change course. Sometimes you need to shake things up, which means messing with your own business creation. Fight the urge to hold on to what's truly not working.

Remember Cindy W. Morrison, who turned a self-published

FOCUS ON SCALE

Melissa Lanz, creator of the Fresh 20 (thefresh20.com), an online meal planning and healthy living service, recommends focusing on scale. "Add a zero to your current sales and challenge yourself to be ready. Think 10, then 100, 1,000, 10,000 and beyond. Look for solutions that could handle such business growth. How can you scale what you're currently offering? What must happen to increase volume to meet that demand?" Posing these questions to yourself often leads to smart decisions and key action steps.

book into a career as a social media strategist? When Cindy discovered her spark, she knew two things: First, she had a large online community of followers who loved to hear tales from her book. Second, talking about her book indefinitely wasn't going to make her the money she needed.

Well-meaning friends and colleagues encouraged her to stick it out. Something would come up, they assured her. Although tempted, Cindy didn't listen. She couldn't because the bills were piling up. When she realized that her initial game plan was no longer a moneymaker, she took stock of what she had in her business arsenal: a passion for helping women reinvent themselves and grow their online presence; a loyal contact list that she engaged with regularly; and a knack for using social media to increase exposure and drive sales.

So Cindy changed her business model. Instead of continuing a conversation about the message in her book—the importance of women supporting one another in times of trouble—she began teaching women how to reinvent themselves, as she had, using social media. She coined a new term: socialvention—reinvention through social media. By recognizing the income limits of her book, she created another, more robust and sustainable, income stream.

DREAM BIG

Rachel Blaufeld, founder of backngroovemom.com, encourages women to not only dream big, but act big as well. "Think about what you want, and be ready to take massive action to turn ideas to reality. Dreaming without doing won't get you what you want."

If you want to grow your business, you've got to be willing to change when you need to. Take stock of the tools you have, the trends and what your clients or prospects are telling you. Use the information to continuously invent and reinvent ways to serve your existing market and new markets, too. If you're standing still and not thinking about your next step, you're opening yourself up to failure. Always keep one eye on the future.

Game On

Your income and influence hinge on your ability to plan big and execute small: big vision for where you want to go, led by small, daily, consistent actions repeated over time.

> **BAN NEGATIVITY**
>
> Elinor Stutz, owner of Smooth Sale (smoothsale.net), a Petaluma, California, company that teaches people how to apply relationship selling to all endeavors, has one firm rule: no downers allowed. "Once I began to ignore negative talk and kept naysayers away from my home, my confidence soared and things took off."

It won't come down to where (or if) you went to school. It won't come down to how much (or how little) money you have in the bank. It won't come down to who you know. It won't come down to the dreams you have. It won't come down to all the noise and chatter. Your bottom line will ultimately come down to what *you do*. It's all about the hustle. Your hustle. No way around it.

Don't get bogged down in assuming you're lacking this, that

or the other. You have exactly what it takes to create the success you envision. Now it's up to you to put it into action.

Let's hustle.

ⅢⅢ act now ⅢⅢⅢⅢⅢⅢⅢⅢⅢⅢⅢⅢⅢⅢⅢⅢⅢⅢⅢⅢⅢⅢⅢⅢⅢⅢⅢⅢⅢⅢⅢⅢ

- How you spend your workday is tied entirely to how successful you'll be in business.

- Stop the information overload.

- Schedule your 5x5: five key things to do every day by 5 P.M. to move your business forward.

- Schedule to-do items with an actual appointment time. Build in two thirty-minute blocks of time for reactive work that pops up unexpectedly.

- Know that "Done!" is often good enough.

- Pounce on the right opportunities and pause on the ones you're not positive about. "Brilliant" but questionable ideas must pass the forty-eight-hour test.

- It's all about the hustle.

a few final thoughts

Nobody is coming to rescue you or your business—it's all up to you. When you need a boost, soak in these ten take-aways and then get to work.

1. **Keep your "why" top of mind always.** Remember your personal rationale for starting this business—the one that makes throwing in the towel impossible.

2. **Set "smart" goals.** Skip pie-in-the-sky generic targets. Go for specific, measurable and time-sensitive goals.

3. **Make BBFs.** Cultivate a core group of Best Business Friends—other entrepreneurs you can depend on for no-nonsense feedback and endless cheering to fuel your success.

4. **Know when to pounce and when to pause.** Don't be distracted by every bright shiny object that comes your way. Determine which opportunities deserve quick action, as well as those that require longer consideration.

5. **Get social.** It's not enough to be "on" Facebook and other networks; you must be actively engaged in daily communication with your

target market. There's no substitute for putting in the time to drive results.

6. **Value your time and talent.** Hours slip away in small business. Track your time and know exactly what it's worth. Not everyone will pay your product or service prices, but that's not an excuse to provide them for free.

7. **Ask, don't hint.** Instead of waiting for the moment to be perfect, speak up when it's good enough. Whether you need help or want to close a sale, be clear and straightforward; no beating around the bush.

8. **Mistakes are teachable moments.** Baseball players make millions, even though they have more misses than hits. If you mess up, learn from it and then keep swinging.

9. **Hustle trumps all.** Your success is not defined by where (or if) you went to school, who you know or how much money lines your bank account. Success will be determined by your hustle—the decisions you make and the actions you take each and every day. You have the ability to do exactly what it takes to get what you want.

10. **Action is the antidote to fear.** Few things are easy and you won't be immune to fear. But smart hustle is the only way to combat worry and make big things happen. Start right where you are—and get moving.

acknowledgments

None of this would be possible without the support of every woman who gave Spark & Hustle a chance. My endless appreciation for your vote of confidence in me and the community we've built together. Andie Avila, my longtime editor at Penguin, was her usual attentive and enthusiastic self as she shepherded this book (our third together), as was my literary agent, Meredith Bernstein. I value the candid counsel of my friend Heidi Krupp, who always pushes me to see bigger than I would on my own. Beth Feldman introduced me to Lifetime Moms (lifetimemoms.com), an exciting partner in Spark & Hustle's expansion. I'm a lucky girl to have so many friends and champions at ABC News, especially the team at *Good Morning America*. I am grateful to Alexandra Hall for wholeheartedly embracing what I wanted to do and where I wanted to go with Spark & Hustle from the minute we met. Special thanks to my mother, Sherry, and brother, David, who never say no, even when my business ideas (and mood) veer off the deep end. And, finally, to Peter and our children, Emma, Jake and Nick: you make every day a dream.

resources

General Resources

fastcompany.com, inc.com, openforum.com, entrepreneur.com
Immerse yourself in smart advice, useful templates and inspiring stories—always ahead of the trends.

sba.gov and score.org
Government resources such as legal, financing and marketing help, along with access to live forums and customized advice.

smartbrief.com
Delivers industry-specific newsletters to your email every day.

Tools and Services

constantcontact.com
This is the service I use to stay in contact with my email subscribers. Email marketing, social media monitoring and event promotion campaigns.

efax.com
Provides a fax number to receive faxes which are delivered to you by email.

google.com/docs
Work on the same documents with your virtual team, assistant or mastermind group.

google.com/voice
Get a free phone number and voice mail for your business.

gopayment.com
Mobile payment solutions to accept credit card payments on the go.

yousendit.com and dropbox.com
Send large files easily via the Web.

surepayroll.com
Online payroll leader for small businesses, plus fresh content weekly on starting and growing a small business with an emphasis on payroll and employee-related issues.

freeconferencing.com and freeconferencecall.com
Host conference calls and teleclasses at no cost.

Coworking

hq.com and loosecubes.com
National resources for affordable options for finding corporate space without investing heavily in your own office, but there are a lot of local coworking options as well.

Funding

indiegogo.com and kickstarter.com
Crowdfunding platforms that allow you to generate cash and buzz for your business or idea by engaging your circle of influence.

kabbage.com, prosper.com and lendingclub.com
With good credit and a solid track record, solicit a loan from peers or online lenders.

Product Development

mominvented.com, jimdebetta.com, edisonnation.com, uspto .gov
Advice and services to take your product idea from concept to shelf.

Website and E-commerce Solutions

paypal.com, constantcontact.com, autowebbusiness.com
Collects payment for events on your website.

e-junkie.com
Solutions for selling products online, especially items available for digital download, like ebooks or audio programs.

wordpress.org, tumblr.com, intuit.com/website-building -software/
Great places to create your website, depending on your skill.

Business Cards

minted.com and moo.com
My vendors of choice for quality business cards.

Self-Publishing Resources

pubit.com and mypublisher.com
My favorite sites for self-publishing and printing beautiful photo books to use as portfolios for your work.

Smartphone Apps

SurePayroll
This mobile app means I don't have to be in the office to pay my team. I can process payroll on the go.

GoPayment
This app from Intuit lets me accept credit card payments at live events. Receipts are texted or emailed directly to customers.

Good Morning America and **ABC News**
These apps keep me in the know with breaking news. Fast updates on the fly.

Evernote
Use this app to clip audio, video, text and images and save them to a central Web repository.

TweetDeck
Connect with contacts across Twitter, Facebook and other social media networks.

Social Media Sites
You should—at a minimum—have profiles created for these major social media sites:

facebook.com

twitter.com

linkedin.com

youtube.com

pinterest.com

google.com/+

tumblr.com

instagram.com

Social Media Resources

animoto.com
Instantly create short videos for promotional purposes using your photos and text.

bitly.com
Shorten and track links, which makes for much cleaner posts (and fewer characters) when you're sharing in social media.

hootsuite.com, roost.com, tweetdeck.com
Tools to streamline and preschedule your social media efforts. (Be cautious about too much automation.)

pagemodo.com
Create a professional landing page for your Facebook fan page.

wildfireapp.com
Create social media contests.

Productivity Resources

evernote.com
Keep notes, screen grabs, articles and websites you want to remember in one place.

tadalist.com and **todoist.com**
Online task managers to stay organized and productive.

timetrade.com
Allow clients or customers to schedule appointments with you via an online calendar.

shoeboxed.com
Convert paper receipts to digital data to organize it for efficient bookkeeping and tax prep.

helpareporter.com
Register for a daily email with queries from reporters, editors and producers looking for expert sources.

Outsourcing

crowdspring.com
Post graphic or other design projects for one hundred thousand creatives to submit their best ideas.

elance.com and **odesk.com**
Access top talent when you have a specific need.

Extensive Spark & Hustle online resources can be found at www .sparkandhustle.com/book.